ONCE UPON A WORD

ONCE *upon* A WORD

A WORD-ORIGIN DICTIONARY *for Kids*

BUILDING VOCABULARY THROUGH ETYMOLOGY, DEFINITIONS & STORIES

JESS ZAFARRIS

ILLUSTRATIONS BY
MARCO MARELLA

callisto
publishing
an imprint of Sourcebooks

TO NANETTE, WHO TAUGHT ME THAT LANGUAGE IS A JOURNEY,
THAT IT'S IMPOSSIBLE TO BE BORED WITH A GOOD IMAGINATION,
AND THAT THE HEART SEES BETTER THAN THE EYES.

Copyright © 2020 by Callisto Publishing LLC
Cover and internal design © 2020 by Callisto Publishing LLC
Illustration © 2019 Marco Marella
Interior and Cover Designer: Emma Hall
Art Producer: Sue Bischofberger
Editor: Erin Nelson
Production Editor: Andrew Yackira

Callisto Kids and the colophon are registered trademarks of Callisto Publishing LLC.

Published by Callisto Publishing LLC C/O Sourcebooks LLC
P.O. Box 4410, Naperville, Illinois 60567-4410
(630) 961-3900
callistopublishing.com

This product conforms to all applicable CPSC and CPSIA standards.

Source of Production: 1010 Printing Asia Limited, Kwun Tong, Hong Kong, China
Date of Production: September 2023
Run Number: 5034843

Printed and bound in China.
OGP 14

CONTENTS

WHERE DO WORDS COME FROM? VI

PART I: WORD JUNGLE 1

ALL WORDS TELL A STORY 2

ROOTS & BRANCHES 5
Latin-Based Roots 6
Greek-Based Roots 12
Prefixes 16
Suffixes 19

FROM ROOTS TO TREES 22

PART II: ETYMOLOGY—FROM AARDVARK TO ZOOLOGY 30

A → Z 32

PART III: WORD PLAY 238

A BELLY FULL OF WORDS 240

NOW THAT'S AN EARFUL! 247

REFERENCES 255

WHERE DO WORDS COME FROM?

Once upon a time, a word was born.

Our story begins more than 1.7 million years ago with the early members of our species, Homo sapiens. They had only recently started making stone tools when they first began giving names to the things they saw, heard, and did.

From here, humans learned to speak, share stories, and pass those stories down. We then came up with symbols to record events, to keep track of all we were learning and doing. The invention of language opened up a new universe of creative expression and imagination. It allowed us to create books, music, and art, to discuss philosophy and make new scientific discoveries.

Although there are some animals, like dolphins and elephants, that appear to have a form of "language," human language remains the most advanced in the known universe.

Learning about the way our ancestors' language grew and changed from simple communication to a world full of different ideas can help us better understand ourselves and each other.

In this book, we'll trace words back to their earliest forms, find out where they came from, and explore what turned them into the terms and phrases we use today. Through etymology, you'll discover the stories behind our language, but first we'll answer two important questions.

WHAT *IS* ETYMOLOGY?

And what does it have to do with learning new words?

Etymology is the study of the way words have changed over time. It looks at where words came from and when they were invented. By understanding word origins, we learn more about how and why the words were first made up. Origins can also tell us more about the places where those words were spoken. Through etymology, we can build our vocabulary and even guess what a word means based on its root. Most importantly, we will learn more about people and cultures from around the world.

Etymologists, or people who study word origins, trace words through history to learn how they came to be. You can think of them as word detectives. They learn about these word histories by reading historical records and documents and comparing the way words have changed over time. Sometimes it can be difficult to figure out exactly what a word's origin or original meaning was, so etymologists make guesses based on the best evidence they can find.

Want in on a little secret? With this book, you can be a word detective too.

FRENCH
ITALIAN
SPANISH
ENGLISH
DUTCH
PORTUGUESE
LATIN
GERMAN
GERMANIC
PROTO-INDO-EUROPEAN

DANISH

NORWEGIAN

SWEDISH

ICELANDIC

OLD NORSE

MODERN GREEK

ANCIENT GREEK

PART I

WORD
JUNGLE

ALL WORDS TELL A STORY

Languages have a history of borrowing from one another. English has diverse origins, with words from dozens of different languages, but most words in English come from four languages: Greek, Latin, Old French, and Old English.

These languages (plus many others spoken in Europe, Asia, and the Americas) are called Indo-European languages. This means they all come from a very ancient single language called Proto-Indo-European. We don't know as much about "proto" languages because there are no written records of them.

However, people who study languages have been able to piece together ideas of what these very early, unwritten languages may have looked like based on the similarities between the languages we speak today. Here's a closer look at how older languages have branched into the modern ones spoken around the world now.

ANCIENT GREEK AND LATIN

Nearly half of all words in the English language have Latin origins. Latin was the language spoken in the ancient Roman Empire. The Roman Empire was very powerful and claimed lands throughout Europe, North Africa, and Western Asia.

When the Romans claimed these lands, their language and culture were often adopted by the people who already lived there. Italian, French, Romanian, Spanish, and Portuguese are all very closely related to the Roman language and are therefore called "Romance" languages. Would you believe that it goes back even further?

The Romans got many of their words from Ancient Greek. Ancient Greek culture played an important role in developing our modern-day sports, science, medicine, philosophy, and politics. The Roman Empire built upon these ideas and spread them throughout Europe. We can thank the ancient Greeks for many of the science and philosophy words we learn about in school today.

OLD ENGLISH

The Anglo-Saxons were a cultural group who lived in Great Britain in the 5th century. Many of our common words come from the language of the Anglo-Saxons, which we call Old English. It originally comes from a much older language group called Germanic, which is also the ancestor of the German, Dutch, and Scandinavian languages.

Old English is an earlier version of our language, but many words in this language are spelled differently and are often unrecognizable to people who speak English now.

For example, the phrase "near and far" was spelled *nean ond feorran* in Old English. There were a few different symbols in Old English, too, like ð and þ, which are now spelled as the two letters "th" today.

OLD FRENCH TO MIDDLE ENGLISH

Between Old English and the English we speak today is Middle English. Middle English was the next stage of the English language that began after the Normans, or people from the region of France called Normandy, invaded England in the year 1066. They brought with them their language, Old French, which blended with the language and customs of the Anglo-Saxons, making Middle English.

Old French was a Romance language, getting most of its words from Latin. Whenever you see a word in this book that has a Latin origin, it's most likely that it was brought to English from Old French. About 90 percent of the Latin-derived words in this book stopped in Old French before they got here!

Middle English words are pretty easy to read and understand if you speak English today, but the spelling was different and changed often because there were no English dictionaries yet.

MODERN ENGLISH

Next came Early Modern English, which was spoken from the 15th century until the 17th century. At the beginning of this period, the printing press made books more common and less expensive, so more people learned how to read and write. As a result, many important books, poems, and plays were created. This introduced new words and phrases into the language. (The first English dictionaries were also written during this time, which standardized spellings and definitions we use today.)

Modern Standard English is what we speak today. The kaleidoscope that is the English language isn't just made up of words that come from Old English, Greek, Latin, and French. Hundreds of words we use come from Arabic sources, and hundreds more are from Native American languages. Everyday phrases and terms also come from Chinese, Japanese, Yiddish, German, Bantu, and so many more.

CHANGING LANGUAGES

Many languages around the world are interconnected—they have borrowed and continue to borrow from one another.

But the sharing of words has often not been a peaceful process. Wars spread the Roman Empire across Europe. And as European explorers sailed to Africa and the Americas, many people were mistreated in the process. Global exploration enriched the English language, but this blending was often the result of conquest. It's important to remember that invaders often took language, culture, and resources in ways that harmed indigenous civilizations.

By studying word history, we learn more about important cultures that were lost or harmed during these conflicts. This knowledge helps us avoid future mistakes while celebrating different ideas, cultures, and languages.

Today, we continue to invent new words whenever we develop new ideas and technology, and even when we make up fun words with our friends. And because communication happens faster than ever, languages can grow and change overnight!

ROOTS & BRANCHES

In order to begin our journey as word detectives, we need to break down words into smaller parts. Many words are made up of roots, prefixes, and suffixes that you can put together like building blocks to make new words. A root is the most basic form of a word. Prefixes and suffixes are word parts you can add to the root to help define it. The prefix comes before a root, and the suffix comes after it.

Some roots are whole words, like *labor*, meaning "work," while others are word parts, like *-lumin-* meaning "light." When prefixes and suffixes are added to roots, longer words are built. Look at what happens when we add prefixes and suffixes to *lumin-* and *labor*.

WORD	PREFIX	ROOT	SUFFIX	MEANING
ILLUMINATION	*il-* "in, on"	*lumin* "light"	*-ation, -tion* "state of being"	the state of being lit up, the state of having light on something
COLLABORATE	*co-* "together"	*labor* "work"	*-ate* "become, do"	to do work together

Here's a secret that not everyone realizes: Prefixes and suffixes are magic. By adding a prefix or suffix to a root word, you can make it change direction, change color, grow, shrink, or even turn into its own opposite! For example, let's take the root word *appear*. If you add the prefix *dis-* to it, you get "disappear." See? We made "appear" disappear just by adding a prefix—just like magic.

The charts on the next few pages show common roots, their Greek and Latin origins, their meanings, and examples. They are followed by some common prefixes and suffixes.

See how many words you can make by adding prefixes and suffixes to the roots!

LITERALLY, DEFINED

In this book, you'll see definitions that include "literal" meanings of words. The definition of a word is the way we use it in a sentence. But when we're studying etymology, we discover the literal meanings of words, or what their origins and pieces meant in older languages.

For example, when we use the word "muscle," we're talking about the body parts that make us strong. It comes from the Latin word for muscle, *musculus*, which is also translated as "little mouse" and comes from the Latin base word *mus*, meaning "mouse." Muscles are named after mice because it was thought that flexing your muscles made it look like mice were crawling under your skin. Even though *musculus* also meant "muscle" in Latin, "little mouse" is the literal meaning of the word.

LATIN-BASED ROOTS

ROOT	LATIN ORIGIN	MEANING	EXAMPLES
AM-	amare, amicus	love, liking, friend	amiable, amateur
AMBI-	ambi	both, on both sides	ambidextrous, ambivalent
ANIM-	anima	breath, life	animal, animation, unanimous
AQU-	aqua	water	aquarium, aquatic

ROOT	LATIN ORIGIN	MEANING	EXAMPLES
BEN-	bene	good, well	benefit, benevolent
CAMP-	campus	field	campaign, champion
CANT-, -CENT-	canere	sing	accent, enchant
CLAM-	clamare	cry out	exclaim, clamor, acclaim
CLAR-	clarus	clear	clarity, declaration
CLUD-, CLAUS-	claudere	close	claustrophobia, include
CREA-	creare	make	create, recreation
CRED-	credere	believe, trust	credible, incredulous
CRUC-	crux	cross	crusade, croissant
CURR-	currere	run, flow	curriculum, currency
DIC-, DICT-	dictare	say, speak	dictator, dictionary
FAC-, FACT-, -FECT-, -FIC-	facere	do, make	perfect, magnificent

ROOT	LATIN ORIGIN	MEANING	EXAMPLES
FIG-, FING-, FICT-	fingere	to form, shape	fiction, figment
FLU-, FLUX-	fluere	flow	fluent
FORT-	fortis	strong	fortify, fortress, fort
FUND-	fundare	found, from the bottom	fundamental
GNOS-	gnoscere	know	agnostic, diagnosis
GRAT-	gratus	thank, please	gratitude, congratulations
IGN-	ignis	fire	ignite, igneous
IMAGIN-	imago	copy	image, imagination
-JECT-	iaciere	cast, throw	reject, trajectory
JUDIC-	iudex	judge	judgment, prejudice
LABOR-	labor	work	labor, collaborate
LEG-, LECT-	legere	choose, gather, read	legend, intelligence
LIBER-	liber	free	liberty

ROOT	LATIN ORIGIN	MEANING	EXAMPLES
LINGU-	lingua	language, tongue	bilingual, language
MAGN-	magnus	great, large	magnificent, magnify
MAL-	malus	bad, wretched	dismal, malevolent, malice
MEDI-, -MIDI-	medius	middle	immediate, medium
MERGE-, MERS-	mergere	dip, plunge	emerge, immerse
MIGR-	migrare	wander	migrate, immigrant
MIN-	minor	less, smaller	minor, miniscule
MIT-, MISS-	mittere	send	transmit, dismiss
MOV-, MOT-, MUT-	movere	move, motion	motivation, motion
NASC-, NAT-	nascere	born	natural, pregnant
NOC-	nocere	harm	innocent, obnoxious
NOMEN-, NOMIN-	nomen	name	onomatopoeia, nominate

ROOT	LATIN ORIGIN	MEANING	EXAMPLES
NOV-	novus	new	innovation, novel
ORDIN-	ōrdō	order	coordinate, extraordinary
PAC-	pax	peace	appease, pacify
PREM-, -PRIM-, PRESS-	premere	press	impress, oppress
PRIV-	privus	own	privacy, privilege
QUER-, -QUIR-, QUESIT-, -QUISIT-	quaerere	search, seek	question, inquire
RID-, RIS-	ridere	laugh	ridiculous, riddle
RUMP-, RUPT-	rumpere	break, burst	eruption, interrupt
SCAND-, -SCEND-, SCANS-, -SCENS-	scandere	climb	ascend, descend
SCI-	scire	know	conscience, omniscient
SCRIB-, SCRIPT-	scribere	write	describe, script
SENTI-, SENS-	sentire	feel	sensitive
SERV-	servare	save, protect, serve	observe, conservation

ROOT	LATIN ORIGIN	MEANING	EXAMPLES
SOL-	solus	alone	desolate, solitary
SPEC-, SPECT-	specere	look	spectator, conspicuous
TEMPOR-	tempus	time	tempo, temporary
TEN-, -TIN-, TENT-	tenere	hold, keep	detention, tenacity
TORN-	tornare	turn	tornado, tournament
TRUD-, TRUS-	trudere	thrust	intrude, protrude
ULTIM-	ultimus, ultra	farthest, beyond	ultimate
VAL-	valere	strength, worth	evaluate, value
VEN-, VENT-	venire	come	adventure, inconvenient
VID-, VIS-	videre	see	improvise, vision
VIV-	vivere	live	survive, vivid

GREEK-BASED ROOTS

ROOT	GREEK ORIGIN	MEANING	EXAMPLES
ACADEM-	akademos	Akadēmos (hero), (Plato's) Academy	academic, academy
ACR-	akros	height, summit, tip	acrobat, acronym
AMPHI-	amphi	both, on both sides	amphibian
ANTHROP-	anthropos	human	anthropology, philanthropy
ARCT-	arktos	bear	arctic, Antarctic
ASTER-	aster	star	astronaut, asteroid, astronomy
-BYSS-	abyssos	bottom	abyss
CENTR-	kentron	center	central, eccentric
CHRON-	khronos	time	chronicle, synchronize
CRIT-, CRISI-	krinein	judge, separate	crisis, critical
CYCL-	kyklos	circle	bicycle, cyclops

ROOT	GREEK ORIGIN	MEANING	EXAMPLES
DACTYL-	aktulos	finger	pterodactyl
DYNA-	dunasthai	power	aerodynamic, dynamite
ECO-	oikos	house	economy, ecosystem
EGO-	ego	self	egocentric
EP-, EPI-	epi	upon, in addition to	episode, epidemic
ERG-, ORG-, URG-	ergon	work	energetic, urgent
GEN-, GON-	genos	birth, kind	genetic, gender
GRAMM-	gramma	letter, writing	anagram, grammar
-GRAPH-	graphein	write, draw	calligraphy, biography
HIER-	hieros	holy, sacred	hierarchy, hieroglyph
HYPN-	hupnos	sleep	hypnotize
IDE-	idea	thought	idea, ideology
KINE-, CINE-	kinein	to move	cinema, kinetic

ROOT	GREEK ORIGIN	MEANING	EXAMPLES
LOG-	logos	word, reason, speech, thought	dialogue, psychology, meteorology
MANI-, MANU-	manus	hand	manufacture, manipulate
MNE-	mnasthai	memory	amnesia, mnemonic
MON-	mónos	alone, only	monastery, monopoly
NAV-, NAUS-	navis, naus	ship	nausea, navigate
NEUR-	neuron	nerve, sinew	neurologist
ODONT-	odontos	tooth	orthodontist
ONYM-	onuma	name	acronym, anonymous, synonym
PATH-	pathos	feeling, disease	sympathy, empathy, apathy
PHIL-, -PHILE	philos	loving	philosophy, bibliophile
PHON-	phone	sound	symphony, telephone

14   ONCE UPON A WORD

ROOT	GREEK ORIGIN	MEANING	EXAMPLES
PHOT-	photos	light	photosynthesis, photograph
PHYSI-	phusis	nature	physical, physics
PLAT-	platus	flat	plateau, platypus
POLI-	polis	city	metropolitan, politics
PROT-	protos	first	prototype
PSEUD-	pseudos	false	pseudonym
PSYCH-	psukhein	mind	psychologist
RHE-	rhein	flow	rhythm, rhyme
SCEPT-, SCOP-	skeptesthai	look at, examine, view, observe	kaleidoscope, microscope
SPHER-	sphaira	ball	hemisphere, sphere
STROPH-	strephein	turn	apostrophe, catastrophe
TECHN-	tekton	art, skill	technology, architect
TELE-	tele	far, end	telephone, telekinesis, telescope

ROOT	GREEK ORIGIN	MEANING	EXAMPLES
THE-	thetos	put	hypothesis, thesaurus
THERM-	thermos	heat, warm	thermostat
TON-	tonos	tone, sound, stretch	baritone, monotony
TOP-	topos	place, location	dystopia, utopia
TOX-	toxon	arrow, bow, poison	toxic
TYP-	tupos	stamp, model	prototype, stereotype
TYRANN-	turannos	terrible, tyrant	Tyrannosaurus, tyranny

PREFIXES

PREFIXES	DEFINITION	EXAMPLES
AB-	away from	abstract, abolish, abyss
AD-, AT-	to, toward	adventure, attention
AN-, A-, AM-, AR-	not, without	anecdote, apathy
ANTI-, ANT-	against, opposed to, preventive	antidote, antagonist

PREFIXES	DEFINITION	EXAMPLES
AUD-	hearing, listening, sound	audience, audible
BI-	two	biscuit, binocular
BIO-	life	biology, antibiotic
CO-, CON- COM-,	with, together	companion, conversation, collaborate
CONTRA-	against	contradict
DE-	down, away from, off	delight, detect
DIA-	across, between	dialogue, diagnose
DIS-	lack of, not	disappear, disgruntled, disgust
ECO-	house	economy, ecology
EN-, EM-	in	embellish, enthusiasm
EU-	well, good	eucalyptus, euphoric
EX-	from, out	excite, exclaim, explore
EXTRA-	outer	extravagant, extraordinary
HYPER-	above, over	hyperbole, hyperactive
IN-, IL-, IM-	in, on	imagine, illuminate, inquisitive
IN-, IL-, IM-	not, un-	independent, illiterate, impossible

PREFIXES	DEFINITION	EXAMPLES
INTER-	among, between	interest, international, interrupt
MULTI-	many, much	multilingual
OMNI-	all	omniscient, omnivore
PAR-, PARA-	beside, near	paragraph, parallel, separate
PED-	foot	expedition, pedestrian, pedigree
PRE-	before	predict, pretend, pregnant
PRO-	before, in front of, forward	protagonist, procrastinate, progress
RE-, RED-	again	reaffirm, redundant, reluctant
RETRO-	backward, behind	retrospect
SUB-	below	submarine
SUPER-	above, over	supersonic, superior
SYN-	with	synonym
TRANS-	across	transparent, transportation
UN-	one	unique, uniform
XEN-	foreign	xenophobia
ZOO-	animal, living being	zoo, zoology

SUFFIXES

SUFFIXES	DEFINITION	EXAMPLES
-ABLE	able, capable	capable, amiable
-ANCE, -ENCE, -ANCY	action, process, state of	alliance, intelligence, brilliance
-ARCH, -ARCHY	ruler	monarch, anarchy
-ATION, -TION	makes verbs into nouns	hallucination, innovation
-ATIVE, -IVE	of or related to; tending to	inquisitive, creative
-CIDAL, -CIDE	killer, a killing	homicide, pesticide
-CY	quality of rank or state	literacy, privacy
-DOM	place, state of being	freedom, kingdom, boredom
-ENS, -ENT	makes nouns and verbs into adjectives	different, ambivalent
-ESE	a native of, the language of	Japanese, Portuguese
-ESQUE	ish, like	picturesque, statuesque
-ET, -LET, -EL, -ELLA	small (diminutive)	umbrella, pocket
-FUL	full of, like	beautiful, delightful

SUFFIXES	DEFINITION	EXAMPLES
-IC, -ICAL	related to, pertaining to	magical, chaotic, acrobatic
-IFY	creates verbs, "to make or cause to become"	magnify, rectify, terrify
-ISM, -SM	belief, method	narcissism, skepticism, enthusiasm
-IST	one who does or makes	botanist, florist, pianist, physicist
-ITE	originating from or derived from, belonging to	dynamite, meteorite
-IZE	become, makes verbs from nouns	recognize, apologize, modernize
-LESS	without	reckless, thoughtless
-LOGY	study of, science	biology, archeology
-MENT	"condition of," makes nouns out of verbs	amazement, enchantment
-METER	measure	kilometer, meter
-NESS	state of being	happiness, business
-NOMY, -OMY	law	astronomy, economy
-OID	like (something else)	humanoid, android

SUFFIXES	DEFINITION	EXAMPLES
-OUS	full of, having to do with, doing, tending to	precocious, mischievous
-PHOBIA	fear of	claustrophobia, arachnophobia
-SPOND	pledge	respond, sponsor, responsible
-TECT	cover	protect, detect
-TION, -ATION, -ION	state, condition, or action	levitation, motivation, navigation, abolition
-TUDE	makes adjectives into abstract nouns	attitude, gratitude
-TY, -ITY	makes a noun out of an adjective	royalty, eccentricity, electricity
-URE	state of, act, process	culture, literature
-Y	characterized by	clammy, happy

THE LONELIEST WORDS

A base word that doesn't exist (or is very rarely used) without a prefix or suffix is called an unpaired word.

For example, we say we are **overwhelmed** or **underwhelmed**, but it's rare to hear someone say they're just "whelmed." Someone can be **reckless**, but what does it mean to have "reck?" You can **debunk** a rumor, but was the rumor "bunked" in the first place?

FROM ROOTS TO TREES

Now that you've seen some of the parts that can be used to make up words, let's think about how to use them.

When I was about ten years old, my dad challenged me to figure out what a word meant based on the parts that made it up. The word he gave me was **ARCHEOFERROEQUESTRIANOLOGIST**. It's a made-up word, but it's made up of real roots, prefixes, and suffixes. At first, it meant nothing to me. The word was so long, it sounded like nonsense! But then he repeated it, saying the different parts slowly: archeo . . . ferro . . . equestrian . . . ologist.

So I thought about each part, and what it could mean when they were put together.

ARCHEO: This part sounded familiar—it was like "archeologist," someone who digs up ancient artifacts and studies old things.

FERRO: My dad is a scientist, and he had taught me that "Fe" was the symbol for the element iron on the periodic table. It's short for *ferrum*, the Latin word for "iron." So "ferro" means "iron."

EQUESTRIAN: Have you ever had friends who learned horseback riding at an equestrian stable? Equestrian is related to horses.

-OLOGIST: Check the previous charts to see if you can guess the meaning of this ending. I had seen this ending on a lot of words for people who are experts that study specific subjects. A psychologist studies the mind. A meteorologist studies the weather. An archeologist studies old things. So, I knew that this ending meant "study" and described someone who is an expert. Let's put all of these together: historic/old + iron + horse + someone who is an expert.

Someone who studies old iron horses? As my dad explained, "iron horse" is a term for an old locomotive, or a big train made of iron. Originally, trains were invented to replace teams of horses that pulled heavy carriages. The earliest trains were even pulled by horses before engines and electric power.

So, an "archeoferroequestrianologist" is someone who studies historic trains.

This little game wasn't just a way to teach me how to dissect made-up words. It was also a way to teach me how to think critically about language. If I could figure out the meaning of words like archeoferroequestrianologist, then I could use this tool to build new words with pieces of words I already knew.

You can do this, too! Flip back to the pages with the charts of roots, prefixes, and suffixes. Take one from each chart, and see what sorts of words you can build using them.

Now test your knowledge and see if you can break these words down into their roots, prefixes, and suffixes and guess what they mean:

· **INQUISITION**

· **ANTHROPOLOGY**

· **MAGNITUDE**

· **INCREDULOUS**

· **TELEKINESIS**

ANSWER KEY

INQUISITION: The process of asking questions about something, from *in-* "in," + *quaerere* "seeking, searching" + *-tion*

ANTHROPOLOGY: The study of humans, from *anthropos* "human" + *-logy* "study of"

MAGNITUDE: Greatness, from *magnus* "great, large" + *-tude*

INCREDULOUS: Not believing, from *in-* "not, un-" + *credere* "believing"

TELEKINESIS: Motion from afar (with your mind), from *tele-* "far, far off" + *kinein* "to move"

UNDERSTANDING ETYMOLOGY

In most definitions in this book, you'll find these key elements:

❶ DICTIONARY

❷ DIK-shun-air-ee

❸ *noun*

❹ A dictionary, like the one you're reading right now, is a book full of words. Dictionaries are arranged in alphabetical order and contain information on what words mean and how to pronounce them.

❺ The word "dictionary" comes from the Medieval Latin *dictionarium*, meaning "a collection of words and phrases." The word was invented around the year 1200 by a teacher named John of Garland. He wrote a book called *Dictionarius* to help his students learn Latin words.

❻ *Dictionarius* was probably a shortening of the full phrase *dictionarius liber*, meaning "a book of words." *Dictionarium* (the noun form of the word) is made up of the Latin *dictio*, meaning "a saying" or "a word," and the ending *-arium*, meaning "a place where [things] are kept." Put together, these parts literally mean "a place where words are kept."

1. The word!
2. Pronunciation: How to say this word out loud. This shows you how each syllable sounds and which one is stressed, or accented.
3. Part of speech: Whether the word is a noun, verb, adjective, adverb, preposition, interjection, or exclamation.
4. Definition: What the word means.
5. Background: Historical information about the word.
6. Etymology: The origins of the word and the reasons why it looks the way it does today.

GROWING YOUR FOREST

While it's fun to impress your friends and teachers by knowing lots of words, learning about etymology isn't just about having a big vocabulary. When you understand the history and meaning of the words you use, you also gain a better understanding of language—and the world! You can be more creative, communicate better, and master new subjects. You can even make up your own new words.

With a strong understanding of etymology, your possibilities are endless. Here are just a few of the ways you can take what you learn in this book and expand on that knowledge.

→ UNLOCK NEW LANGUAGES

Etymology can help you understand the meaning of words that you've never seen or heard of before just by looking at them—even words in other languages! English is made up of words derived from Latin, Greek, French, Spanish, Italian, German, Dutch, Swedish, Arabic, Native American languages—and more! With knowledge of roots and word origins, you can learn any of these languages more quickly.

→ BECOME AN UNSTOPPABLE WORD EXPERT

Reading can seem like a tricky obstacle course when you run into a word you've never seen before. But with an understanding of etymology, there's no word that can stop you. Any time you see a long word with many letters, break it down into parts and see if you can guess what each part means, just like we did in the previous section. Before you know it, you'll be able to guess the meaning of the word perspicacious (to have good judgment), and you'll be a regular sesquipedalianist, or someone who uses really long words.

→ TACKLE ANY SUBJECT

When you can guess the meaning of any word, you can read any book. Even the most challenging subjects won't be out of your reach.

In fact, etymology can help you learn these new subjects quickly. As we know, many common words in science, technology, philosophy, and law come from Latin and Greek. You'll approach these subjects already knowing what the difficult words mean.

The library will be your gateway into endless stories and learning.

→ BECOME A GRAMMAR WIZARD

Etymology can help you understand grammar more easily. Once you understand common roots, prefixes, and suffixes, you'll get a better understanding of different parts of speech and the elements of sentences. Look back at the suffix section above. What happens when you add the ending -ous to the noun "mischief"? You get "mischievous," which is an adjective. Suffixes can help you change words from one part of speech to another.

→ TRAVEL THE WORLD—AND THROUGH TIME

With an understanding of etymology, you have the power to travel through time and learn more about different civilizations.

In the next section, you'll see that the Old English word for "game" was *gamen*, which comes from a root meaning "people together." That tells us that the Anglo-Saxons valued their time together, playing games. You'll also see that the Greeks and Romans valued their gods and mythology and often named things after them, including things like "cereal," "money," and "inspiration."

Learning about etymology is like having a superpower that helps you see through portals to new and old places and cultures.

→ TAKE A JOURNEY IN SOMEONE ELSE'S SHOES

Languages are built through connections. By studying the origins of words, you can see how ideas and words spread throughout the world over time.

Many of our words that relate to sports and physical feats—like "marathon" and "acrobat"—come from the Olympic Games that were originally held in Ancient Greece. These games have spread throughout the world, becoming global traditions that everyone can celebrate.

→ INVENT NEW WORDS—AND INVENT NEW *WORLDS*

William Shakespeare was a poet and a playwright, and many consider him to be one of the greatest wordsmiths in the English language. He invented hundreds of words using pieces of words from Old English, Latin, and Greek. Sometimes he changed a word's part of speech, making nouns out of verbs and vice versa. Here are just a few words that Shakespeare is credited with inventing: coldhearted, eventful, swagger, fitful, squander, multitudinous, dwindle, misquote, and uncomfortable.

And Shakespeare isn't the only one who did this. In the Harry Potter series, J. K. Rowling built the names of people and places using etymology: Headmaster Albus Dumbledore's name is built from Latin and Old English words meaning "white bumblebee," and the villain Voldemort's name means "flight of death" in French.

Like these writers, you can build worlds and fill them up with creative characters just by using some etymological magic of your own.

A YEAR OF WORD ORIGINS

The calendar we use today is called the Gregorian calendar. It was named after Pope Gregory XIII, who wanted calendars to be based on the position of the sun throughout the year. The Catholic church often used Roman and Greek words and ideas to build their own rules, and our modern calendar is no exception. Although our months are named after Roman and Greek words and names, their timing is a result of Roman months blending with other calendars. The old Roman calendar, used before 46 BCE, began in March.

The list below shows the origins of the months on your calendar.

In Latin, some months were called "the month of _____." For example, what we call February was called *februarius mensis*, or "the month of purification."

JANUARY – from the name of Janus (*Ianuarius* in Latin), two-faced Roman god of doorways, changes, beginnings, and endings.

FEBRUARY – from the Latin *februare,* meaning "to purify." This was the last month of the ancient Roman calendar and was a time for renewal. In Old English, the name for the second month of the year was *solmonað*, supposedly meaning "mud month."

MARCH – from the name of Mars, Roman god of war.

APRIL – origin uncertain, but possibly from the name of the Greek goddess Aphrodite, or from a root meaning "the following" or "the next" because it was the second month of the ancient Roman calendar.

MAY – origin uncertain, but possibly from the name of *Maia*, a Roman earth goddess.

JUNE – from the name of Juno, Roman goddess of women and marriage. In Old English, it was called *liðe se ærra*, meaning "earlier mildness."

JULY – from the name of the Roman ruler Julius Caesar, who was born in the fifth month of the year, originally called *Quintilis*, meaning "fifth." It was renamed after his death, and later shifted to the seventh month.

AUGUST – named after the Roman emperor Augustus Caesar.

SEPTEMBER – from the Latin *septem*, meaning "seven," because it was the seventh month of the Old Roman calendar. Originally named *Germanicus* after a Roman emperor, but it didn't stick.

OCTOBER – from the Latin *octo*, meaning "eight," because it was the eighth month of the Old Roman calendar. Originally named *Domitian* after a Roman emperor, but it didn't stick either.

NOVEMBER – from the Latin *novem*, meaning "nine," because it was the ninth month of the Old Roman calendar. The Old English name for this month was *Blotmonað*, or "blood month," because it was a time when animals were sacrificed and stored for food in winter.

DECEMBER – from the Latin *decem*, meaning "ten," because it was the tenth month of the Old Roman calendar.

PART II

ETYMOLOGY—
FROM
AARDVARK
TO ZOOLOGY

30

ACROBAT

Read more on page 34

A

AARDVARK   *ARD-vark*   *noun*

An aardvark is a mammal that eats insects and looks like a pig with a long nose and tail. Its name means "earth-pig," from the Afrikaans Dutch *aard*, meaning "earth" or "dirt," and *vark*, meaning "pig," because this animal burrows into the earth and resembles a pig.

ABOLISH   *uh-BAH-lish*   *verb*

To abolish something means to make it illegal or put an end to it. It comes from the Latin word *abolere*, which means "to grow away from." The prefix *ab-* means "off, away from," and the older word *adolere* means "to grow."

Example: The fifth-grade student body president helped abolish the use of single-use plastics in her school.

ABSTRACT   *AB-stract*   *adjective*

Abstract can mean something that you can't experience with your five senses, like the idea of freedom. It can also refer to an art style that doesn't show a recognizable image. Have you ever seen a colorful canvas with shapes, paint splatters, and lines, but without people or objects? That's probably abstract art. The word comes from the Latin *abstractus*, meaning "drawn or moved away," which is formed of the prefix *ab-*, meaning "off" or "away from," and *trahere*, meaning "to draw, drag, or move."

ABYSS   *uh-BISS*   *noun*

An abyss is a deep pit or space that seems to go on forever and you can't see the end. It comes from the Greek word *abyssos*, which combines the prefix *a-*, meaning "without," and *byssos*, meaning "bottom."

ACADEMIC   *ak-a-DEM-ic*   *adjective*

Something that is academic involves education, learning, or scholarship. The word comes from the name *Akademeia*, the garden where the famous Greek philosopher Plato taught his students. The Akademeia grove was named after the legendary hero Akademos, who was rumored to be buried there.

ACCENT   *AK-sent*   *noun*

Your accent, or the way you pronounce words, usually depends on where you or your family live or came from. For example, Americans pronounce the English word "clever" differently than people from England and Australia. Even people who live in different regions of the same country might have different accents. Think of the difference between the way people talk in Tennessee and the way they talk in New York.

The word comes from the Latin *accentus*, which means "song added to speech." It's formed from the prefix *ad-* and *cantus*, or "singing." But why? After all, accents appear in regular speech, not just songs.

In Ancient Greece and Rome, stories were often told in verse, which means that they were arranged to have rhythm to them, like a chant or a song.

ACCIDENT   *AK-sid-ent*   *noun*

An accident is something that happens by chance, instead of being planned. The Latin word *accidentem* means the same thing. The base word *cadere* means "to fall," giving the full word the sense of something that "befalls" you, or "falls upon" you.

ACCUSE   uh-KYOOZ   *verb*

To accuse someone of a wrongdoing is to blame them for it. Like many words that have to do with crimes and laws, it comes from Latin. The word *accusare* specifically meant "to bring to trial."

Example: My brother accused me of eating all his candy—but I only had one piece!

ACHIEVEMENT   uh-CHEEV-mint   *noun*

An achievement is something won or completed. Maybe you achieved a good grade in your class, or your team achieved victory in a game. It comes from the Old French *achever*, meaning "to complete" or "to finish." The term originally comes from the Latin phrase *ad caput*, which means "to come to a head," or "to reach its end or highest point." In English, the phrase "to come to a head" means that a problem has reached its highest point and must be solved right away.

ACROBAT

AK-roh-bat

noun

An acrobat is someone who puts on an amazing gymnastic performance in a circus or on stage. Many acrobats perform high in the air on a trapeze or tightrope. Acrobat means "one who goes to the top" or "one who walks high up," from the Greek *akros*, meaning "height," the "tip of a peak," or the "top of something high up," and *bainein*, meaning "to go" or "to walk." It's related to the Greek *akrobatos*, a word for walking on your tip-toes or climbing up high.

ADOBE   uh-DOH-bee   *noun*

Adobe is a type of sunbaked brick material used to build houses and other structures. It is usually a mixture of clay, straw, and mud. The word is Spanish, meaning "mudbrick," and originally comes from the Arabic *al-tob*, "the brick."

ADVENTURE   *ad-VEN-chur*   *noun*

When we think of adventure today, we might think of pirates and epic journeys. But the word "adventure" used to simply mean anything that happens by chance or luck. It comes from the Latin phrase *adventura res*, which means "a thing about to happen." It took on the meaning of "an exciting incident or occurrence" or "an account of marvelous things" later, after people began writing and telling exciting fictional stories of things that happened by chance.

AERODYNAMIC   *AIR-oh-dye-NAM-ik*   *adjective*

Aerodynamics is the study of how well things can move through the air. Something that is aerodynamic, like an airplane or a smooth, slim sports car, can move quickly and easily without much drag or resistance from the air. A broad and blocky shape is not aerodynamic because it would be slowed down by resistance from the air as it moves. This is why planes are designed as long, slim tubes. The word "aerodynamic" is made up of the Greek elements *aero*, meaning "air," and *dynamikos*, meaning "power."

AGNOSTIC   *ag-NOSS-tik*   *adjective*

Someone who is Muslim, Jewish, or Christian believes in God, and someone who is an atheist believes there are no gods. But someone who is agnostic believes that we can't ever be sure whether a god exists or not. It comes from the Greek *agnostos*, meaning "unknown" or "unknowable," made up of the prefix *a-* or "not," and *gnostos*, or "known."

ALARM   *uh-LARM*   *noun/verb*

A security alarm, an alarm clock, or the alarm bell that warns people of a fire drill gets its name from the Italian military cry *all'arme*, meaning "To arms!" or "Get to your weapons!" Italian soldiers would shout this phrase when they needed to rally each other to defend castles and military bases.

    Bonus fact: The word "arms" is another name for "weapons." It comes from the Latin word *arma*, which literally meant "tools," but specifically came to refer to tools used for war.

ALBATROSS   *AL-buh-tross*   *noun*

The famous island prison Alcatraz is named after the Spanish and Portuguese word for this long-winged white seabird. Etymologists aren't sure exactly which word it came from, but it was definitely Arabic—likely *al-ghattas*, meaning "sea eagle."

ALCHEMY   *AL-kuh-mee*   *noun*

Alchemy was what people called chemistry before modern times. It was also a word used for the process of trying to turn one type of material, like lead or iron, into a more expensive and rarer one, like silver or gold. It comes from the Greek *khemeioa*, but the origin of the Greek word isn't quite as clear. It either comes from the Greek *khymatos*, meaning "that which is poured out" (as you might pour out a chemical mixture or potion), or from *Khemia*, which is the name Greeks used for the region we now call Egypt, where much of our early knowledge of chemistry and medicines came from.

ALGEBRA   *AL-juh-bruh*   *noun*

The area of mathematics we call algebra was invented by ancient Babylonians as early as the second century BCE. The word comes from the Arabic word *al-jabr*, which was used by an Iraqi mathematician to mean "a reunion of broken parts." In fifteenth-century English, "algebra" referred not only to mathematics but also to the process of setting broken bones.

ARABIC WORD ORIGINS

You'll notice that many words that begin with *al-* come from the Arabic language. That's because the prefix *al-* is the definite article in Arabic, meaning it is the Arabic word for "the."

ALLIGATOR *AL-lih-gate-or* noun

Alligators are large reptiles that live both in water and on land. Their name comes from the Spanish term *el lagarto de Indias*, meaning "the lizard of the Indies." The English word evolved from just the first two words in the Spanish phrase, so "alligator" literally means "the lizard." Even though they look like giant lizards, today we know that alligators aren't lizards at all, but are a completely different kind of reptile.

ALLITERATION *al-LIT-er-ay-shun* noun

Alliteration is a term for a series of words that all start with the same letter or sound. "Ben bakes bread better than Barry" is a sentence using the letter "b" as the alliteration. Alliteration can also be based on the *sounds* the letters make. "Kangaroos can quickly catch clever koalas" is an example of alliteration. The word was created by Italian poet and historian Giovanni Pontano, based on the Latin *alliterare*, meaning "to begin with the same letter."

ALLY *AL-liy* noun/verb

We often think of allies as countries or people that support one another's causes, especially in war. A long time ago, the verb "ally" simply meant to get married to someone. Allies were your family and relatives, from the Old French word *alier*, meaning "combine" or "unite." The word "ally" became more connected with the military during World War II, when England, America, the Soviet Union, and France joined together with other countries and called themselves the Allied Powers, who opposed the Axis Powers (Germany, Italy, and Japan).

ALOOF *uh-LOOF* adjective

To be aloof means to act in an unfriendly, cold, or distant way. This word was first a nautical term—a word associated with the ocean and ships. Sailors used *loof*, a Dutch word, to mean the direction in which the wind blew. These sailors would steer the ship *aloof*, or headed into the wind, in order to stay *distant* from rocky shores.

AMATEUR   *AM-uh-choor*   *noun*

An amateur does something as a hobby rather than for money. An amateur guitarist plays guitar for fun at home, but doesn't play in concerts; an amateur painter makes paintings for their friends and family, rather than for a museum or gallery. The word was adopted from French, and it originally comes from the Latin *amatorem*, meaning "lover." After all, to be an amateur, you have to love your hobbies so much that you don't mind doing them just for fun or outside of school.

AMAZE   *uh-MAYZ*   *verb*

To be amazed is to be dazzled or stunned by something you've seen or heard. Its root is the Old English *mæs*, which has the same meaning as the word "maze." The puzzle games we call mazes today were named after the word's original meaning, "a state of confusion or bewilderment." So, in a sense, to amaze someone is to drop them in the middle of a confusing mental maze!

AMBIDEXTROUS   *am-bee-DEKS-truss*   *adjective*

Can you write well with both your right and left hand? Then you might be ambidextrous! That means that you aren't right-handed or left-handed, but can use both hands equally. It comes from the Latin word *ambidexter*, which means "right-handed on both sides." The word *dexter*, or "right-handed," is also the source of the word "dexterity," the quality of having quick, graceful, and skillful hands, like a juggler. Lots of people are left-handed too, including famous artists, musicians, inventors, and world leaders. Leonardo da Vinci, Wolfgang Amadeus Mozart, and Alexander the Great were all left-handers!

AMBIVALENT   am-BIH-vah-lent   adjective

Ambivalence, or to be ambivalent, means that you don't feel strongly about picking between two choices. It was first used in the study of emotions. Psychologist Paul Eugen Bleuler invented the word, which means "strength on both sides," building it with the Latin elements *ambi-* "both" or "on both sides," and *valentia*, meaning "strength."

Example: My mom asked me if we should eat pizza or pasta for dinner. I'm ambivalent because I like both!

AMIABLE   AY-mee-ah-bull   adjective

The Latin word *amicus* means "friend" or "loved one." This word forms the origin, or root, of "amiable," which means friendly and helpful, just like a friend.

AMNESIA   am-NEE-zhee-uh   noun

Amnesia is another word for losing your memory. It comes from the Greek *amnesia*, meaning "forgetfulness," from the prefix *a-* or "not," and *mnasthai*, meaning "to remember."

Example: After I fell off my bike and hit my head, I had amnesia. I couldn't remember what happened for a whole week before the accident!

AMPHIBIAN   am-FIB-ee-an   noun

Most animals that live on land (like humans and dogs) breathe using their lungs. Most animals that live in the ocean (like fish and sharks) breathe using gills. An amphibian is an animal, such as a frog or a salamander, that does both at different stages of its life. For example, a frog starts out as a tadpole that lives in the water and breathes through its gills like a fish. It then grows into an adult frog that lives on land and breathes with its lungs. The word comes from the Greek *amphibios*, meaning "living a double life," which is made up of *amphi*, meaning "both," and *bios*, meaning "life."

AMYGDALA   *uh-MIG-duh-luh*   *noun*

The amygdala is an important part of your brain that helps you remember things, make decisions, and feel emotions. It comes from the Greek *amygdale*, meaning "almond," because it's shaped like an almond. It's no wonder some people say that when you're thinking cleverly, you're "using your nut"!

ANACONDA   *an-uh-CON-duh*   *noun*

Anacondas are huge snakes that live in tropical areas of South America. Etymologists aren't sure exactly where these gigantic snakes got their name. The best guess about this word's origin is that it's from Sri Lanka. The Sinhalese or Sri Lankan word *henacandaya* means "whip-snake" or "lightning-stem."

ANAGRAM   *AN-uh-GRAM*   *noun*

An anagram is a word whose letters can be mixed up to make another word. For example, "silent" is an anagram of "listen" because they contain all of the same letters, just in a different order. Some anagrams are words that make different words when you read them backward: "Evil" read backward becomes "live." Anagram is made up of the Latin prefix *ana-*, meaning "back" or "backward," and *gramma*, meaning "letter."

ANARCHY   *AN-ar-key*   *noun*

A monarchy has a monarch, or king or queen, leading the state; a democracy is ruled by representatives elected by the people. But anarchy is a state of chaos where there is no recognized leader, or the people decide to ignore the leadership. This word come from the Greek *anarkhos*, or "rulerless," which is made up of the prefix *an-*, meaning "not" or "without," and *arkhos*, meaning "leader."

ANATOMY   *uh-NAT-uh-mee*   *noun*

Anatomy is the study of and the shape of the human body. It comes from the Greek word *anatomia*, which means "dissection" or "a cutting up." Early scientists would open bodies to learn from them, and this led to the formation of the modern-day term. In the 1500s, people also used the word "anatomy" to refer to mummies and skeletons.

ANECDOTE   *AN-ek-doht*   *noun*

An anecdote is a short, personal story about something that happened to you. If you're sharing an anecdote about dogs, you would tell a short and funny story about your dog. Anecdotes can be made up, too. The word comes from the Greek term *anekdotos*, which means "not published." (When you publish something, like a book, you make it public to read.) *Anekdotos* was originally the name of a book full of (previously unpublished) stories of silly things that happened to a Byzantine ruler.

Example: My science teacher shared a funny anecdote about a time when she dyed her fingers blue during a chemistry experiment.

ANIMAL   *AN-uh-mul*   *noun*

Are you a plant? No. Are you a mineral? No. How about a fungus? Not so much. You're an animal, just like cats and parrots and whales. The word comes from the Latin *anima*, meaning "breath," "life," or "spirit" because animals move, breathe, and live their lives.

ANIMATE   *AN-uh-MATE*   *verb*

If you've ever seen a cartoon or computer-animated movie, you've watched an animation—a picture that moves. This word literally means "to bring to life," also from the Latin *anima*, meaning "breath," "life," or "spirit."

ANTHROPOLOGY   *AN-throw-PAW-loh-jee*   *noun*

Anthropologists study the history and culture of humans from many different times and places. They study people alive today—and our ancestors! The word "anthropology" is made up of the Greek *anthropos*, meaning "human being," and *-logy*, meaning "study of."

ANTIDOTE   *AN-tih-doht*   *noun*

An antidote is medicine that cures you if you consume something harmful. The word comes from the Greek phrase *antidoton pharmakon*, which means "a remedy" or "a drug given against something," from the elements *anti*, meaning "against," and *didonai*, meaning "to give."

APATHY   *A-puh-thee*   *noun*

Apathy means to not care about something. It comes from the Greek word *apatheia*, which means "without emotion." When you break this word down more, *pathos* means "emotion" or "feeling," so putting the prefix *a-*, which means "without," in front of it, it means "without emotion."

Example: My partners for the group project in history class didn't care about their grades, so I did most of the work on it. I felt frustrated by their apathy.

APOLOGY   *uh-PAW-low-jee*   *noun*

Have you ever had to apologize for something? Today, we think of it as saying sorry. But to the Greeks, an apology was something you said to defend yourself or your opinions. Debate was an important aspect of Ancient Greek culture, much like it is today. When someone disagreed with you back then, you would make an *apologia*, or a speech to stand up for your ideas. The Greek word is formed from the elements *apo*, meaning "away from," and *logos*, meaning "speech." Together they mean "speaking away from."

APOSTROPHE   *uh-PAW-stroh-fee*   *noun*

An apostrophe can do two things: It can show belonging or posses-sion, as in "Melissa's dog" (the dog that belongs to Melissa) or "Fred's mother" (the mother of Fred). It can also show that letters have been removed, as in "haven't" (short for "have not") or "they've" (short for "they have"). The word "apostrophe" comes from the Greek *apost-rephein*, meaning "to turn away," which is made up of *apo*, meaning "off, away from," and *strephein*, meaning "to turn." The idea is that the symbol "turns away" or sends away the letters that are removed from the original word.

AQUATIC   *a-KWAH-tik*   *adjective*

Aquatic animals and plants are those that make a splash! In other words, they live in water. Their name comes from the Latin word for water, *aqua*. The word "aquarium," or fish tank, comes from the same source.

Example: Coral reefs in the ocean are home to many aquatic plants and animals.

ARCTIC   *ARK-tik*   *adjective*

Have you ever looked up in the night sky to see the constellation called the Big Dipper? Another name for it is Ursa Major, which means "the greater she-bear." The word "Arctic," referring to the North Pole, comes from the Greek word *arktos*, which meant "of the north" but was also literally a word for "bear." The Greeks named the north after the bear constellation because it is always visible in the northern polar sky. Thanks to what we know about the prefix *ant-*, we can guess that "Antarctic" (the South Pole) means "opposite the bear."

Example: Polar bears live in the Arctic region near the North Pole. Most types of penguins live in the Antarctic region near the South Pole.

ASTEROID   *ASS-ter-oyd*   *noun*

An asteroid is a type of very small, rocky planetoid. It's formed of the Greek elements *aster*, meaning "star," and *eidos*, meaning "form or shape." So, asteroid means "star-shaped" or "starlike." (That's also why starfish belong to the class Asteroidea.)

ASTRONAUT   *ASS-troh-not*   *noun*

Do you dream of space travel? You might want to become an astronaut when you grow up. We know from the word "asteroid" that the prefixes *aster-* or *astro-* mean "star." The second part of this word, "naut," comes from the Greek *nautes*, or "sailor." So, an astronaut is literally a "star sailor."

ASTRONOMY   *uh-STRON-uh-mee*   *noun*

Astronomy is the science of outer space. It comes from the Greek word *astronomos*, which means "the regulation of the stars." It is made up of the elements *astron*, "star," and *nomos*, which means "regulating, or law."

ATTENTION   *uh-TEN-shun*   *noun*

When you pay attention to your teachers, you are listening to what they have to say. "Attention" comes from the Latin *attendere*, which means "to listen to" but literally translates as "to stretch toward." This "stretching" sense comes from the fact that you are directing your mind, ears, and focus toward the teacher.

ATTIC   *AT-tik*   *noun*

The word "attic" comes from the name of Attica, a region near Athens, Greece. The Greeks didn't usually have attics—storage areas at the top level of a house—like the ones we do today, but in classical Athenian architecture, many structures had pointed roofs. This left a small triangular space above the columns—room for decorations! Today, we still have pointed roofs on our houses, but we use that extra triangular space to store things (and sometimes build forts!).

AUDIENCE   *AW-dee-ence*   *noun*

What do you do when you're sitting in the audience? You're probably watching, but most importantly, you're listening. The word "audience" comes from the Latin word *audentia*, which means "listening." Back in the times of kings and queens, if you asked for help, they would "grant you an audience." This meant they would listen to your troubles.

ORIGIN SPOTLIGHT: *AUDIRE*

Review the definition of these three words that come from the Latin *audire*.

- **AUDIBLE:** Able to be heard.

- **AUDIOBOOK:** A book you can listen to.

- **AUDIENCE:** A group of people who listen to and watch a performance.

What do they have in common? Can you guess what *audire* means based on these definitions?

If you guessed "to hear" or "to listen," you're right! All of these words rely on your sense of hearing.

AWKWARD   *AWK-word*   *adjective*

Have you ever felt embarrassed because you did something silly? You might have felt a little bit awkward. (We all do sometimes!) This word originally came from an Old Norse word meaning "turned the wrong way." You might recognize the *-ward* ending from words like "toward" and "backward." This ending adds direction to a word. In this case, "awkward" suggests something pointed in the wrong direction.

BUOY

Read more on page 51

B

BAMBOOZLE   *bam-BOO-zull*   *verb*

Have you ever played a prank on a friend—or had a prank played on you? To bamboozle someone is to trick them. Etymologists aren't quite sure where it came from, but some suggest that it came from Scottish slang words like *bombaze* or *bumbaze*, meaning "to perplex." Others think it came from the French word *embabouiner*, which means "to make a baboon of someone," or to make them look silly and foolish.

Example: The magician bamboozled the audience by making a card disappear. In truth, she slipped the card up her sleeve!

BANDICOOT   *BAN-duh-coot*   *noun*

A bandicoot is the name of several species of Indian and Asian rats known for their destructiveness and large size. Its name is an English version of the Telugu (a language native to India) word *pandi-kokku*, meaning "pig-rat."

BARBARIAN   *bar-BAIR-ee-an*   *noun*

The word "barbarian" comes from the Medieval Latin word *barbarinus*, a word for anyone who wasn't Roman or Greek. The root *barbar-* was used to imitate the unintelligible speech of foreigners, so essentially, "barbarian" means "a person who says 'blah, blah, blah.'"

BARRICADE   *BAIR-uh-kaid*   *noun/verb*

Soldiers and rebels build barricades to block off streets or to protect bases during battles. "Barricade" literally means "made of barrels," from French and Spanish origins, because during a riot or a big public uproar, people fighting would set up blockades or a wall made of barrels filled with rocks and dirt. Today, we use the word informally, too. You can barricade your door with pillows or your treehouse with a pile of leaves.

BENEFIT   *BEN-uh-fit*   *noun/verb*

A benefit, or something beneficial, is something that helps (or benefits) you or someone else. It comes from the Latin *benefactum*, meaning "good deed." It is made up of the elements *bene*, meaning "well," and *facere*, meaning "to do."

BENEVOLENT   *buh-NEV-oh-lint*   *adjective*

Someone who is benevolent is kind, gives to other people, and works for the greater good. Adopted from Old French, it originally comes from the Latin *benevolentem*, meaning to wish that good things will happen to someone else. It's from *bene*, or "well," and *volantem*, "to wish." When you swap *male* (meaning "badly") for *bene*, you get "malevolent," which means to wish bad things upon someone.

BEYOND   *bee-YOND*   *preposition*

If something is "beyond" your house, it means it's past your house, or on the other side of it. "Beyond" comes from the Old English word *begeondan*, which means "on the other side of." You might recognize the "yond" portion of the word from "yonder," which people usually say when they mean "over there."

BIBLIOPHILE   *BIB-lee-oh-file*   *noun*

If you're reading a book about etymology, you are probably a biblio-phile, or someone who loves books. The first element of this word is *biblio-*, or "book," from the Greek *biblion*, meaning "paper" or "scroll." The second part, *-phile*, means "lover," from the Greek *philos*, meaning "loving" or "dear."

BINOCULARS   *bih-NOK-yoo-lars*   *noun*

Have you ever looked through a pair of binoculars? The Latin prefix *bi-* means "two," and *ocularis* means "eye." This tool lets you see far away through two short telescopes—an extension of your two eyes!

BIOLOGY   *bi-AWL-oh-jee*   *noun*

At some point, you'll probably take a biology class in which you'll study animals, plants, and the human body. The prefix *bio-* means "life," and it appears in many English words including biodegradable, biography, and biopsy. If we combine this prefix with the ending *-logy*, meaning "science" or "theory," we get the meaning "the science of life."

BIZARRE   *bih-ZAR*   *adjective*

"Bizarre" comes from the Italian word *bizzarro*, a word that describes someone who is cranky or tends to have quick flashes of anger. Over time, the word *bizzarro* softened its meaning to mean "unpredictable," "strange," or "weird." It was adopted in French, which we then borrowed in English.

BLADE   *BLAYD*   *noun*

We tend to think of swords and knives when we think of blades. But it also applies to a much smaller, usually green object. The Old English word *blæd* meant "leaf"—or a blade of grass. It could also refer to anything leaf-shaped, like an oar or the head of a shovel.

BLAZE   *BLAYZ*   *noun/verb*

This word, which is usually associated with a huge fire, comes from an early Germanic root meaning "shining" or "white." It can refer to dancing flames, but "blaze" is also a word for the white spot that many horses have on their foreheads. The saying "to blaze a trail" means to create a physical path or lead people down a new path. It usually means you're the first, in some aspect, to do something. This concept comes from the fact that pioneers would make notches, or blazes, in tree bark as they made their way through unexplored forests so that they could find their way back, and others could follow.

Example (verb): Young people like Greta Thunberg are blazing the trail for environmental justice.

BOOK   *BUK*   *noun*

To understand the origin of this word, we need to look back to the living things from which books are made: trees! "Book" comes from a Proto-Germanic root meaning "beech tree." This is probably because writing tablets were once made from beechwood. Similarly, the Latin word *librum*, also the word for "book," originally meant "the inner bark of trees."

BOTANICAL   *buh-TAN-uh-kul*   *adjective*

Have you ever been to a botanical garden? It's a special kind of garden or park where many plant species are grown. You can think of it as a zoo or museum for plants! "Botany" comes from the Greek word *botane*, which could mean any type of plant, but most often refers to grass that farmers would feed to cows and sheep. In fact, the related word *boton* means "grazing beast."

BRAIN   *BRAYN*   *noun*

No one is quite sure of the exact origin of the word "brain," but one guess is that it comes from a root meaning "broken." We usually think of "broken" as something being damaged or needing to be fixed, but in this case it refers to the wrinkles, curves, and hemispheres of our brain that make it look like it's broken into segments. It's this beautiful "brokenness" that makes us able to think, feel, and create!

BRILLIANT   *BRILL-yant*   *adjective*

"Brilliant" describes things that are dazzlingly bright or sparkling— literally "shining like beryl," from the Latin *berillus*. Beryl is a brightly colored mineral and gemstone that comes in several varieties, including emeralds and aquamarine. To say that a person is brilliant is to say that their intelligence and cleverness shine as brightly as one of these colorful gems.

BUFFOON buh-FOON noun

If you puff up your cheeks with air, you'll be pantomiming (or play-acting) the origin of "buffoon." It isn't a common insult anymore, but it was once used to mean anyone foolish or absurd, or specifically a jester or comic fool. It comes from the Italian *buffare*, meaning "to puff out the cheeks," just like a jester would in a comedic performance.

BULLY BULL-ee noun/verb

Did you know that being a bully was once a good thing? Today, "bully" is a word for a cruel person or the act of being cruel, but in the 1500s, people used it to mean "sweetheart," referring to both men and women. It probably comes from a Germanic word for "lover" or "brother." The meaning likely changed to refer to someone pushy or mean because the word sounds a lot like "bull," a big male cow that can be very stubborn and moody.

BUOY

BOO-ee

noun

A buoy is a floating object placed in the ocean to warn boats and ships about areas in the water that are dangerous or shallow. It likely comes from a Proto-Germanic root meaning "signal" or "beacon," or perhaps from an Old French word for "chain" because buoys are usually attached to the ocean floor by chains. Because buoys float, the adjective "buoyant" refers to something that floats or the emotional state of feeling light and happy.

BUSINESS BIZ-uh-ness noun

When we grow up, our jobs can keep us very busy. That's why business means exactly what it looks like: *busy-ness*. It comes from the Old English *bisignes*, which meant anything that you cared about or kept you occupied.

CARIBOU

Read more on page 54

C

CALLIGRAPHY   *kuh-LIG-ruh-fee*   noun
Calligraphy is a special kind of decorative penmanship or handwriting. It is considered a visual art. Calligraphy comes from the Greek *kaligraphia*, which is formed of *kallos*, meaning "beauty," and *graphein*, meaning "to write."

CAMOUFLAGE   *KAM-uh-fladj*   noun/verb
"Camouflage" refers to paint and other materials used to disguise people, army machinery, and animals. It comes from the Italian *camuffare*, "to disguise," and was adopted in French as *camoufler* before it was used in English.

Example (noun): A tiger's stripes are good camouflage when it's hunting in tall grass.

CAMPAIGN   *kam-PAYN*   noun/verb
You've probably heard of a political campaign, when someone running for office tries to get people to vote for them. "Campaign" is also a word for the movement of an army onto the battlefield. It comes from the Old French word *champagne*, meaning "open country," where two armies might meet for battle. (Champagne is also the name of a French city that has wide open fields where they make bubbly wine.) Originally, the word comes from Latin, with the base word *campus* meaning "field."

CANOE   *kuh-NOO*   noun
A canoe is a lightweight boat that you steer and propel with paddles. The boat's design and name both come from the indigenous people of Haiti. In Arawakan, the indigenous language of Haiti, this boat is called a *canaoua*.

CAPABLE   *KAPE-uh-bull*   *adjective*

You can do it! To be capable means to have the ability to do something. This word overlaps with the word "capacity," which means the ability to hold or do something. A large cargo ship, for example, has a high storage capacity. Your mind also has a large capacity for learning new skills. Both come from the Latin *capax*, meaning "able to hold much."

Example: My brother got the flu, so he was not capable of finishing his homework.

CARGO   *KAR-goh*   *noun*

Today, cargo is anything carried in storage in a car, ship, plane, wagon, or train. It was adopted from the Spanish *cargo*, meaning "burden." Its origin refers to the vehicle that carries this stuff—the Latin *carrus* means "wagon," and is also the source of the English word "carriage."

CARIBOU
KAIR-uh-boo

noun

A caribou is a large type of reindeer. Its name is an Algonquian (Native American) word meaning "pawer" or "scratcher" because it digs in the snow with its hooves to find moss and grass.

CARPENTER   *KAR-pen-tur*   *noun*

This name for a professional woodworker is from the Latin *carpentum*, which meant "wagon," "carriage," or "cart." In Latin, an *artifex carpentarius* was a person who made wooden carts. In English, "carpenter" replaced the Old English word *treowwyrhta*, literally "tree-wright." A "wright" is someone who makes or builds something: A playwright creates plays for the theater, a shipwright is someone who builds ships, and a tree-wright would be someone who makes things from wood.

CARTOGRAPHY   *kar-TOG-ruh-fee*   noun

Cartography is the art and science of making charts and maps. If you break it down, it literally means "the drawing of maps," formed of the Latin *carta* or *charta*, which could refer to a piece of paper, a card, or a map, and the Greek *-graphein*, meaning "to write" or "to draw."

CARTOON   *kar-TOON*   noun

The word "cartoon" is much older than the animated shows you might watch. It is derived from the Medieval Latin *carta*, or "paper." At first, "cartoon" was a name for the heavy paper that artists, especially newspaper cartoonists, used for their early sketches. Over time, the word referred to the drawings themselves, and eventually to hand-drawn animations.

CATAPULT   *KAT-uh-polt*   noun

A catapult is a machine that uses a lever to throw heavy things into the air. Large catapults were used to attack castles and fortresses, propelling rocks and other large objects at high walls to knock them down. The Greek word for catapult was *katapeltes*, which is composed of *kata*, meaning "against (a wall)," and *pallein*, meaning "to toss or hurl."

CATASTROPHE   *kuh-TASS-troh-fee*   noun

Today we think of a catastrophe as a horrific event. Its original meaning was a little less dramatic. It was once a word for "a reversal of what is expected," or the opposite of what you think will happen. "Catastrophe" comes from the Greek *katastrophe*, meaning "an overturning," "a sudden end," or a "turning downward." The Greek word is made up of the elements *kata*, meaning "down," and *strephein*, meaning "to turn." It makes sense that "catastrophe" came to mean "disaster" over time because when something like a hurricane comes, it can overturn buildings!

CATERPILLAR   kat-ER-pill-er   noun

The word "caterpillar" originally comes from the Latin words *catta*, meaning "cat," and *pilosus*, meaning "hairy, shaggy, or covered with hair." It literally means "shaggy cat"! The Old English term for these insects was *cawelworm*, or "cole-worm." "Cole" was a Middle English word for cabbage, and caterpillars love to eat cabbages! English isn't the only language where "caterpillar" refers to other animals. The French word for caterpillar, *chenille*, literally means "little dog." In some Italian dialects, caterpillars are called *gattola*, or "little cat." In Portuguese, the word for caterpillar, *lagata*, comes from the Latin *lacertus*, meaning "lizard."

WHY DO SOME WORDS SOUND FUNNY?

Some words sound funnier than others. This happens for several reasons. Funny-sounding words may be onomatopoetic. Onomatopoeia refers to a word that sounds like its meaning. Take **cackle**, for instance: This word for a witchy laugh also sounds like someone laughing when you say it out loud. It was originally a word for a chicken's clucking—and sounds a bit like that, too. **Squelch**, meaning to squish something, also sounds like the noise you hear when you step in something squishy, like mud. Other examples include **sizzle**, **bonk**, **thud**, and **twang**.

These words have imitative origins, meaning they exist because someone turned the sound into a word. Many of these words are thought to sound funny because it can be unexpected to hear someone say a word that copies a silly sound effect.

Uncommon letter combinations can also sound funnier than expected ones. Dr. Seuss is famous for inventing nonsense words that sound silly for these reasons. He created rhymes with words like "rumbus," "sneedle," "vipper," "schlupp," and "grickily gructus." These words are not only nonsensical but are also made of less common letter combinations.

What are some of the silliest words you know? Can you think of more examples of onomatopoeia?

CEMETERY   *SEM-it-ary*   *noun*

A cemetery is a plot of land used to bury and honor people who have passed away. It comes from the Greek *koimeterion*, meaning "sleeping place." It is formed from the words *koiman*, meaning "to put to sleep," and *keimai*, meaning "I lie down."

CHALLENGE   *CHAL-inj*   *noun/verb*

"Challenge" comes from the Old French *chalongier*, meaning "complain, protest, haggle." It originally comes from the Latin *calumnia*, meaning "trickery." In English, the word originally meant to yell at someone or blame them. In olden times, when someone was blamed for doing something, they had to defend themselves to a judge or fight in a duel. This is where we get the meaning of the word today—something to face or overcome.

CHAMELEON   *kuh-MEE-lee-un*   *noun*

A chameleon is a type of lizard that can change its color to match its surroundings. Its name literally means "lion on the ground," from the Greek *khamai*, meaning "on the ground," and *leon*, meaning "lion." This is probably because some chameleon species have a crest on their necks that looks like a lion's mane.

CHAMPION   *CHAM-pee-yon*   *noun*

A champion is a person or team member who wins a tournament or contest. Adopted from Old French, this word originally referred to a fighter who was victorious on the battlefield. It comes from the Latin *campionem*, meaning "a fighter in the field," with the base word *campus*, or "field."

CHAOS   *KAY-oss*   *noun*

"Chaos" once meant "emptiness" or "nothingness." It comes from the Greek *khaos*, meaning "abyss" or "that which is vast and empty." Today, it means confusion and disorder, because it was once thought that the nothingness in the universe had no order or reason to it before the planets came to be. Scientists now know much more about our planetary systems!

CHARISMA   *ker-IZ-muh*   *noun*

A person who has charisma has an outgoing, charming personality and gets along well with other people. The Greeks believed this personality trait was a gift from the gods, which is the meaning of the original Greek word *kharisma*. The base word, *kharis*, shows us that those gifts include "grace," "beauty," or "kindness." They even had a goddess named Charis!

CHARITY   *CHAIR-uh-tee*   *noun*

If you give your time or money to charity, you are helping those who need something like food, shelter, or water. We get this word from the Old French *charité*. This word had the same meaning, but also meant "compassion," because giving to others requires love and compassion. Its original source is the Latin *carus*, meaning "dear," "valued," or "loved."

CHIMPANZEE   *CHIM-pan-ZEE*   *noun*

Did you know that chimpanzees are humans' closest relatives? Scientists say they might even be as smart as young human children! Chimps raised by humans have been taught sign language and common human skills. The name of this intelligent species of apes was adopted from West African languages, perhaps the Vili word *cimpenze* or the Tshiluba word *chimpenze*, both of which mean "ape."

CHINCHILLA   *chin-CHILL-uh*   *noun*

A chinchilla is a fluffy rodent that's similar in size to a rabbit. It has shorter ears and a longer tail. Its name in Spanish literally means "little bug" and may originally come from the Latin *cimicem*, meaning "bedbug."

CHRONICLE   *KRON-ik-ull*   *verb*

To chronicle something is to write it down as a story or history. You may recognize the word from C. S. Lewis's book series *The Chronicles of Narnia*, a story about the fictional land of Narnia. This word originally comes from the Greek word *khronos*, meaning "time" because chronicles share things that happened over a period of time.

CHUCKLE   *CHUK-ull*   *verb*

If you listen closely, when some people laugh, they sound like chickens! This happens if they're chuckling or laughing in a low or quiet way. The word comes from the Middle English word *chukken*, meaning "to make a clucking noise."

CLAIRVOYANT   *klare-VOY-ent*   *noun/adjective*

Someone who is clairvoyant is thought to be able to see into the future. Clairvoyants are also sometimes called psychics, oracles, or soothsayers. This word was adopted directly from French and means "clear-sighted," from the elements *clair*, meaning "clear," and *voir*, meaning "to see."

CLARITY   *KLARE-ih-tee*   *noun*

Clarity is a state of being easy to understand. If your teacher provides clarity on a math problem, it means they are explaining it in a way you can understand. "Clarity" can also be a word for clearness, like the clarity of a diamond or a very clean window. This word comes from the Latin *claritas*, meaning "brightness," "clearness," or "splendor." It is originally from *clarus*, meaning "clear."

CLAUSTROPHOBIA *KLAW-stro-foh-bee-uh* *noun*
Claustrophobia is the fear of being in tight or closed spaces, from
the Latin *claustrum*, meaning "a place shut in" or "a closed place,"
and *-phobia*, meaning "fear."

CLIMAX *KLY-max* *noun*
The climax is the part of a story when the action, emotion, or tension
reaches its most intense and dramatic peak. For example, in the fairy
tale *Cinderella*, the climax occurs when Prince Charming slips the glass
slipper onto Cinderella's foot. Because it is the height of the story,
the word "climax" derives from the Greek word *klimax*, which literally
means "ladder."

CLONE *KLOHN* *noun*
"Clone," comes from the Greek *klon*, meaning "twig." That's because the
earliest clones were actually plants. Farmers would cut off twigs from
mature, healthy plants and use them to grow new plants. When scientists began to experiment with cloning more complex organisms, like
sheep, they used the same word to describe the process of creating
genetically identical individuals.

COIN *KOYN* *noun*
"Coin" comes from the Latin *cuneus*, or "corner." When the word first
arose in English in the early fourteenth century, it meant "wedge." It
quickly came to mean "thing stamped" or "a piece of money" because
the tools used for stamping metal were wedge-shaped.

COINCIDENCE *KOH-in-sid-ents* *noun*
When two things unexpectedly happen at the same time, that's a coincidence. The word comes from the Medieval Latin *coincidere*, meaning "to
fall upon together." Broken down, this word actually has two prefixes: *co-*,
or "together," and *in-*, which means "upon" in this case. These prefixes are
added to the base word *cadere*, or "to fall."

COMEDY   *KOM-id-ee*   noun

"Comedy" implies something funny today, but that wasn't always the case. Before the sixteenth century, a comedy wasn't necessarily funny. It was simply a word for a play or story with a happy ending. (This was different from a tragedy, which has a sad ending.) Comedy is derived from the Greek *komodios*, which refers to actors or singers in any entertaining performance, from *komos*, meaning "festival or merrymaking," and *aoidos*, meaning "singer or poet."

COMET   *KOM-it*   noun

Comets are chunks of frozen rock, gases, and dust that create a bright trail, or "tail," when they fly closer to the sun. "Comet" comes from the Greek *kometes*, which means "long-haired," because the comet's fiery tail looks like a long trail of hair.

COMPANION   *kum-PAN-yin*   noun

A companion is a friend or family member who sticks with you through thick and thin. From the Latin *com-*, meaning "with" or "together," and *panis*, meaning "bread," a companion is literally someone you eat bread with. This is also the same origin as "company." In Ancient Rome, there were strict rules about hospitality. When someone came over to your house, you were obligated to provide them with food (to "break bread" with them)! The custom was to open your home, offer entertainment, and even give gifts.

CONGRATULATE   *kon-GRAT-yoo-LAYT*   verb

To congratulate someone (or say "congratulations") is to wish them well for something good. You might congratulate a friend on graduating from middle school, or your grandparents on their anniversary. This word is built from the Latin prefix *con-*, meaning "together," and *gratus*, meaning "thankful," "pleasing," or "agreeable." After all, when you congratulate someone, you're telling them that you're happy for their good news—you're celebrating together.

CONSCIENCE   *KON-shence*   *noun*

Your conscience is the voice inside your head that tells you what's right and wrong. The word's origin also suggests something shared. The Latin *con-scientia* means "a joint knowledge of something." The idea is that you know something is wrong because there is a collective, or group, understanding of what makes something okay or not okay.

Example: I lied about how much Halloween candy I ate and had a guilty conscience.

CONSERVATION   *KON-serv-ay-shun*   *noun*

Conservation refers to the important process of protecting nature and wildlife. It comes from the Latin *conservare*, meaning "to keep, preserve, or guard." This is made up of the prefix *con-*, meaning "together," and *servare*, meaning "to keep watch."

CONSPICUOUS   *kon-SPIK-yoo-us*   *adjective*

Something conspicuous is not hidden, but very eye-catching and easy to see. It comes from the Latin *conspicere*, meaning "to notice" or "to observe," from the prefix *con-* and *specere*, meaning "to look at." The prefix *con-* usually means "together," but in this case it is used to make the word *specere* stronger. We can look at something eye-catching together!

Example: The traveling circus was conspicuous in every town.

CONTRADICT   *KON-truh-dikt*   *verb*

To contradict someone is to disagree or argue with them. Two things that are contradictory are opposites. It comes from the Latin phrase *contra dictere*, meaning "to speak against."

CONVERSATION   *KON-vur-say-shun*   noun

A conversation is when you talk with people. It originally comes from the Latin *conversare*, meaning "to turn about together." This is made up of the prefix *con-*, meaning "together," and *vertere*, meaning "to turn." Much like a dance, you and another person talk about things centered around the same topic.

COORDINATE   *koh-ORD-in-ate*   verb

To coordinate with someone is to do something at the same time as them. To coordinate an event is to make sure that everything happens when and where it's supposed to. This word comes from the Latin *coordinare*, meaning "to arrange" or "to put in order." It is made up of *co-*, meaning "together," and *ordo*, meaning "arrangement" or "row." When you're coordinating, you're putting things together or in a row.

COWARD   *KOW-erd*   noun

A person who is a coward lacks the courage to do brave things. The word "coward" comes from the Old French *coart*, meaning the tail of an animal, and *-ard*, a negative ending that usually indicates something unpleasant. In this case, it suggests that the animal's tail is tucked in fear. The suffix is also used this way in words like "braggart" and "buzzard."

CRAVE   *KRAYV*   verb

When you're craving a particular kind of food, it's almost like your body is demanding to have it. It should be no surprise that "crave" comes from the Old English *crafian*, meaning "to ask for earnestly" or "to demand by right."

CREATE   *kree-AYT*   *verb*

Whether it's art, music, or basketball plays, creating allows you to bring something new into the world. "Create" and "creative" are derived from the Latin *creare*, meaning "to make or bring forth." The Latin word is also closely related to the concept of motherhood—creating a new life and bringing it into the world.

Example: The islands that make up Hawaii were created by volcanoes that erupted from under the Pacific Ocean.

CRITICAL   *KRIT-uh-cull*   *adjective*

To be critical is to look closely at something and make decisions about it. Critical thinking is an important part of learning more about a subject. The words "critical" and "critic" originally come from the Greek *krinein*, meaning "to separate" or "to decide."

CROCODILE   *KROK-uh-dyle*   *noun*

"Crocodile" most likely comes from the Greek *krokodilos* (*kroke* "pebbles" + *drilos* "worm"). The word was used to describe crocodiles who lived in the Nile and basked on the pebbly shore. When children pretend to cry just to get what they want, it's said that they are crying "crocodile tears." These fake tears are named after the fact that crocodiles can cry tears that have nothing to do with their emotions.

CRUSADE   *kroo-SAYD*   *noun/verb*

A crusade is an organized and energetic effort to achieve something. To "go on a crusade" is to passionately go after something, but it's not usually used in a positive way. It was originally the name of military efforts that took place from the 11th to the 13th centuries when Christian European armies tried to claim "Holy Land" from Muslim people who had claimed it before that. The European armies marched under banners with crosses on them, and that's where the word "crusade" comes from: the Latin *crux* means "cross."

Example: The school nurse went on a crusade to ban chocolate milk.

CRYPTIC   *KRIP-tik*   *adjective*

Something that is cryptic is mysterious or puzzling. It might have a hidden meaning. It makes sense that its Greek source, *kryptos*, means "something hidden or concealed."

CULTURE   *KULL-chur*   *noun*

Culture is the way people act, speak, and express themselves, often through music and art. Every civilization on earth has had customs that represent a collective culture. The word comes from the Latin *colere*, meaning "to tend, guard, or cultivate." In early human history, people were nomads, traveling to find food and resources. The first towns and cities were built after people began to create farms and stay in one place. It was here that the earliest cultures were tended, guarded, and cultivated.

CURFEW   *KUR-fyoo*   *noun*

When you go out in the evening, your parents might give you a curfew, or a time when you need to be home. In 14th-century English, it was spelled "curfeu" and referred to a bell or signal that would ring when it was time for people to extinguish their fires and lights for the night. This was a common practice intended to prevent accidental fires from starting after people fell asleep. Its Old French origin, *cuevrefeu*, literally meant "to cover the fire."

CURIOUS   *KYUR-ee-us*   *adjective*

Someone who is curious is inquisitive or eager to learn. It can also mean something strange and unusual. It is derived from the Latin *curiosus*, meaning "full of care." This makes sense in both cases. You are either learning something with great care or you must pay something that is out of the ordinary great care.

CURMUDGEON *kur-MUDJE-un* *noun*

A curmudgeon is a bad-tempered older person who is grumpy and miserly, meaning he or she isn't very giving or charitable. The word's origin is uncertain, but one theory is that it comes from the French phrase *coeur mechant*, or "wicked heart." Another possibility is that it comes from the Gaelic *muigean*, a word for an unpleasant or disagreeable person.

CURRENCY *KUR-en-see* *noun*

Currency is any system of money used to exchange for goods and services. In America, the U.S. dollar is the official currency. Most countries in Europe use the Euro. In Morocco, the basic unit of currency is the dirham. There are many different types of currencies around the world. In fact, some people use the word "currency" to describe a barter. If you have three ripe oranges and your friend has one slice of cake, to exchange for the cake you might use your oranges as currency. The key is that currency holds enough value to allow for a swap. Currency "flows" from one person or business to another—and that's where its name comes from. Its Latin origin *currere* means "run" in the same way a river runs.

CURRICULUM *kur-RIK-yoo-lum* *noun*

The classes you need to graduate are organized to make a curriculum. The curriculum is designed like a path, with one class leading to another to help you learn everything you need to know in the right order. The word was adopted straight from Latin and literally means "a running." You advance through your classes like you might run on a path or in an obstacle course. The activities you participate in outside of the classroom are called "extracurricular" activities, adding the Latin *extra*, or "outside." You can think of your extracurricular hobbies as your outside path!

CYCLOPS   *SIY-klops*   *noun*

A cyclops is a mythical giant from old Greek stories that has only one big, round eye. The most famous cyclops was named Polyphemus. The word originally comes from the Greek *kyklops*, meaning "round-eyed," which is made up of *kyklos*, meaning "circle," and *ops*, meaning "eye." *Kyklos* is also the source of words like "cycle" (something that turns in a circle), "bicycle" (which has two circular wheels), and "cyclone" (which turns in a circle).

Read more on page 78

D

DACHSHUND *DOK-sund* *noun*

Dachshunds, also known as wiener dogs, are known for their long bodies and short legs. Despite their size, they were bred to hunt badgers. Their name means "badger hound" in German. Their short legs made them small enough to chase badgers into their burrows.

DAISY *DAY-zee* *noun*

The name of this flower comes from the Old English word *dægesege*, which meant "day's eye." This is because the petals of some daisy species open when the sun rises and close when the sun sets.

DANDELION *DAN-duh-liy-on* *noun*

The word "dandelion" comes from the French name for the flower, *dent de lion*, which literally means "lion's tooth." This refers to the shape of its pointed leaves. This common weed has also had a variety of other names, including "tell-time," "cankerwort," and "milk witch."

DANGER *DAIN-jur* *noun*

In the Middle Ages, the word "danger" had a completely different meaning than it does today. At that time, it meant "arrogance" or "power." It comes from the Old French *dangier*, which meant "power" or "control" to harm someone else. It was this "harming" factor that turned the word into what is means today: something perilous, risky, or to be feared.

DECIDE *de-SIDE* *verb*

When you can't make a decision, it's almost like you're debating or arguing with yourself. When you finally decide, you put a stop to that internal arguing, or cut it off. The Latin origin, *decidere*, literally means "to cut off," formed of *de-*, meaning "off," and *caedere*, meaning "to cut."

DECIDUOUS   *duh-SID-joo-us*   *adjective*

Deciduous trees have leaves that change color in the autumn, compared to evergreen trees, whose leaves remain green all year. Maple, oak, and beech trees are deciduous trees. But did you know this word shares an origin with the word "decay"? Both come from the Latin *decidere*, which means "to fall off" or "to fall down." In the case of deciduous trees, the leaves change color and then fall off.

DECLARATION   *DEK-lur-ay-shun*   *noun*

The Declaration of Independence was signed by the founders of the United States on July 4, 1776. It declared that the United States was an independent nation that couldn't be controlled by the British government. A declaration is a formal statement or announcement. It comes from the Latin *clarus*, meaning "clear," because when you declare something, you want to make it clear to everyone. In most cases, the prefix *de-* means "down" or "away from," but in this case it's what we call an intensifier—it makes the base word stronger. To add *de-* to *clarus* makes it not just clear, but also *very* clear.

DEFY   *dee-FYE*   *verb*

To defy an order is to decide not to obey it. To defy someone is to reject that they are in charge. It originally comes from the Latin *disfidare*, meaning "to renounce one's faith." The Latin root *fidus* means "faithful."

DELIGHTFUL   *duh-LYTE-full*   *adjective*

Based on what we know about prefixes and roots, the word "delight" looks like it should mean "away from light," or "unlit," which doesn't sound so delightful. The spelling of this word changed after it was adopted from the Old French *delitier*, meaning "to please greatly or charm." The origin of the "light" portion of the word is the Latin *lacere,* meaning "to lure or entice." This is also the source of the word "delicious."

DEMOCRACY   *duh-MOK-ruh-see*   *noun*

A democracy is a type of government in which power belongs to the people. In a democracy, laws are passed through representatives who are voted in by their constituents (people in their district or hometown). In Greek, *demokratia* literally means "rule by the people." This is formed from *demos*, meaning "common people," and *kratos*, meaning "rule or strength."

Example: When I went to Capitol Hill to watch representatives vote, I got to watch democracy in action!

DEMOLISH   *deh-MAWL-ish*   *verb*

To demolish something is to destroy it. As we know, the prefix *de-* can mean "down," but what about the second part of the word? The Latin word *moliri* means "to build or construct," so to demolish something, especially a building, is to literally "build it down"—that is, to deconstruct it or tear it down.

DESCEND   *duh-SEND*   *verb*

To descend a set of stairs is to walk down them. To descend in an elevator is to ride it down. The word comes from the Latin *descendere*, meaning "to come down" or "to sink," literally "to climb down." It is made up of the prefix *de-*, meaning "down," and *scandere*, meaning "to climb."

DESCRIBE   *duh-SCRIYB*   *verb*

To describe something is to explain it to someone else. You might describe the way your dog looks to your friend, or you might describe the way it feels to go on a fun roller coaster. You can describe something out loud or in writing. This word comes from the Latin *describere*, meaning "to write down," from the prefix *de-*, meaning "down," and *scribere*, meaning "to write."

DESOLATE   *DESS-oh-let*   *adjective*

A desolate place is empty and bare, such as a deserted town with no people living in it. This word comes from the Latin *desolare*, meaning "to leave completely alone." In this word, the prefix *de-* is an intensifier, meaning that it makes the base word extra powerful. When you add the prefix to the base word *solare*, or "to make lonely," it turns the meaning into "to make completely lonely."

Example: The landscape in the Sahara Desert is desolate, with very few people, animals, or plants living amid the hot, sandy dunes.

DETECTIVE   *duh-TEKT-ive*   *noun*

A detective is someone who investigates by "detecting." They find clues and follow them to solve a crime. To detect literally means "to uncover" the truth, from the Latin *de*, "off, away from" and *tegere*, meaning "to cover."

DETENTION   *dee-TEN-shun*   *noun*

Have you ever gotten detention in school? This word comes from the Latin *detinere*, meaning "to hold back" or "to keep off." It is from the prefix *de-*, meaning "away" or "off," and *tenere*, meaning "to hold." When you get detention, your school holds you back from other activities after class, or keeps you away from recess or free period.

DIAGNOSE   *DIY-ug-nohss*   *verb*

When you're not feeling well, you hopefully get to tell a doctor what you're feeling. They will study your symptoms, then use their knowledge to diagnose your illness. To diagnose something is to reveal the cause of something. Doctors spend many years studying biology to make correct diagnoses, but they're not the only ones. Teachers study students to diagnose learning challenges. Businesspeople diagnose problems to make a profit. The word "diagnose" reflects that knowledge. Its two Greek sources (*dia*, meaning "between," and *gignoskein*, "to learn" or "to come to know") combine to mean "to know thoroughly."

DIALOGUE   *DIY-uh-log*   noun

Dialogue can refer to a conversation in a story, a play, or between two people talking in real life. It's formed of the Greek components *dia*, meaning "across, between," and *legein*, meaning "to speak."

DIARY   *DIY-uh-ree*   noun

Many people who keep a diary try to write in it every day. The word comes from the Latin *diarius*, meaning "daily."

DICTATOR   *DIK-tay-tur*   noun

A dictator is a leader with absolute authority. The word comes from the Latin *dictare*, from a source meaning "to speak" or "to say." A dictator is a leader who dictates the law, in other words, their word is the law.

DICTIONARY   *DIK-shun-air-ee*   noun

A dictionary, like the one you're reading right now, is a book full of words. Dictionaries are arranged in alphabetical order and contain information on what words mean and how to pronounce them. The word "dictionary" comes from the Medieval Latin *dictionarium*, meaning "a collection of words and phrases." The word was invented around the year 1200 by a teacher named John of Garland. He wrote a book called *Dictionarius* to help his students learn Latin words. *Dictionarius* was probably a shortening of the full phrase *dictionarius liber*, meaning "a book of words." *Dictionarium* (the noun form of the word) is made up of the Latin *dictio*, meaning "a saying" or "a word," and the ending *-arium*, meaning "a place where [things] are kept." Put together, these parts literally mean "a place where words are kept."

DINOSAUR   *DYNE-uh-soar*   *noun*

"Dinosaur" comes from the Greek words *deinos*, which can mean "wondrous" or "terrible" (producing fear), depending on how much you like dinosaurs. *Sauros*, the other root, means "lizard." For many years, paleontologists believed that dinosaurs were giant lizards, which we now know is not true. While lizards and dinosaurs are both classified as reptiles and share a common ancestor, dinosaurs are a different type of reptile.

DIPLOMA   *dih-PLOH-muh*   *noun*

When you graduate from school, you will receive a diploma, or a document showing that you completed your studies. It was borrowed directly from Greek, though Greeks also used it to refer to government documents. The literal meaning of diploma is "paper folded double," from the Greek *diploun* "to double, fold over." This word is also the source of "diplomat," a government official who makes agreements and treaties with other countries (usually on double-folded paper in Ancient Greece), and "diplomacy," which is the art of dealing with people who disagree with you or one another.

DISASTER   *diz-ASS-tur*   *noun*

Remember the word *aster*, meaning "star"? That root origin makes sense for words like "astronaut" and "asteroid," but you might not expect that "disaster" also comes from *aster*. Adding on the prefix *dis-* gives this word the meaning "an ill-starred event." In ancient times, many people believed (and some still do) that the position of the stars could cause good and bad things to happen. If the stars were in an unfavorable position, it was believed to be an omen that disaster was sure to strike!

DISGRUNTLED   *dis-GRUN-tuld*   *adjective*

If you're disgruntled, you're angry or dissatisfied. You might even grunt and grumble! In certain English dialects in the Middle Ages, "gruntle" was a word for a pig, originally from the Old English *grunnettan*, or "to grunt," an imitative word. Pigs tend to make low grunting sounds when they're happy or satisfied, so to be disgruntled means the opposite—to be an unhappy pig, or to be in a bad mood.

DISGUISE   *dis-GIYZ*   *noun*

A disguise is a costume that conceals your identity. Adopted from the Old French *deguiser*, the word literally means "away from one's appearance," from *des-*, meaning "away" and *guise*, meaning "style or appearance."

DISMAL   *DIZ-mull*   *adjective*

If you're feeling dismal, you're having a very bad day. Based on what we know about prefixes, you might think that it includes the prefix *dis-*, "opposite" or "away from," but the word "dismal" is unusual. It comes from the Medieval Latin phrase *dies mali*, literally "evil days" or "bad days." During the medieval era, a dismal day was thought to be cursed or unlucky.

DISMISS   *diss-MISS*   *verb*

When class is dismissed, you're allowed to leave. This word comes from the Latin *dimittere*, meaning "send away," from the prefix *dis-*, or "away," and *mittere*, meaning "to send."

DISORIENT   *dis-OR-ee-int*   *verb*

To be disoriented is to be confused because you don't know where you are or what direction you're going. The first element, *dis-*, means "not" or "lack of." The second part, "orient," means to figure out which direction is which. This part comes from the Latin *orientem*, meaning "the east," which itself is from *oriri*, meaning "to rise." A compass can tell you which direction is which, but if you're lost without a compass, the easiest way to tell what direction you're facing is to watch the sun. It rises in the east and sets in the west. When the sun rises, you can tell which direction east is and then "orient" yourself by figuring out the other cardinal directions.

DIZZY   *DIZ-ee*   *adjective*

The word "dizzy" evolved from the Old English *dysig*, meaning "foolish." Its earlier origins may imply dust, vapor, or smoke, because the feeling of being dizzy makes your head feel clouded.

DODO   *doh-doh*   *noun*

The dodo was a species of flightless birds from Mauritius Island in the Indian Ocean. These birds went extinct in the 1600s after they were overhunted by Dutch and Portuguese sailors. The birds were large, slow, awkward, and unafraid of people, so the sailors believed them to be very unintelligent. The origin of the word is uncertain, but it most likely comes from the Dutch word *Dodaars*, which referred to the knot of feathers on the birds' tails. Other possible origins are the Dutch *dodoor*, meaning "sluggard" (a slow or lazy person), or the Portuguese *doudo*, meaning "fool or simpleton."

DOLPHIN   *DOLL-fin*   *noun*

"Dolphin" is related to the Greek *delphys*, meaning "womb," probably due to the fact that dolphins are mammals that give birth to live offspring, rather than laying eggs like most fish and crustaceans.

DOODLE   *DOO-dul*   *noun/verb*

A coodle is a drawing made by someone who isn't paying full attention to their sketch. Doodling can be a fun, creative exercise! But if you're doodling during class, there's a good chance you're not paying attention or are just trying to pass the time. "Doodle" was probably inspired by "dawdle," meaning "to waste time." Someone who doodles acts like a "daw," a type of crow known for its playful and silly behavior.

DRAGON   *DRAA-gun*   *noun*

Dragon comes from the Latin *draconem*, meaning "huge serpent." Before that, it came from the Greek *drakon*, which meant "great sea serpent." The Greek word comes from an even earlier Proto-Indo-European root meaning "to see." In a literal sense, *drakon* was "the one with the deadly glance." Never try a staring contest with a dragon!

DRIZZLE   *DRIZ-ull*   *noun/verb*

When it isn't raining heavily, but tiny droplets of water are falling like a mist, we say that it's "drizzling." There are two theories about this word's origin, both from Middle English. It might be from *drysning*, meaning "a falling of dew." Or it could be from *dresen*, simply meaning "to fall."

DROWSY   *DROW-zy*   *adjective*

Have you ever felt so drowsy, or sleepy, that you found your eyelids and head drooping? Drowsy comes from the Old English *drusan*, meaning "sink," suggesting someone sinking into sleep.

DUBIOUS   *DOO-bee-us*   *adjective*

To be dubious is to be uncertain or doubtful, perhaps because you cannot make a decision. Both "doubt" and "dubious" come from the Latin *dubitare*, meaning "to question, hesitate, or waver in opinion." The idea of being undecided between two choices appears in the base word, *duo*, which means "two." It gives the words the sense of being "of two minds," or choosing between two options.

DUDE

DOOD   *noun*

Dude, what's the origin of the word "dude"? Today, "dude" is a slang word that is interchangeable with "guy" or "man"—it can even be genderless and refer to anyone. But in the 1800s in New York City, "dude" meant a very well-dressed and tidy man, also called a "dandy." This was possibly inspired by the popular folk song "Yankee Doodle." After that, in the early 1900s, "dude" came to refer to city-dwelling tourists who would travel west on vacation. The ranches that welcomed these tourists came to be known as "dude ranches." Over time, the word became more fun and casual.

DYNAMITE

DIY-nuh-miyt

noun

A stick of dynamite can create a very big explosion. This explosive material was invented by the Swedish scientist Alfred Nobel, who made it so that builders could blast through rock and mountains in order to make roads and bridges more easily. The word comes from the Greek word *dynamis*, meaning power.

ENTOMOLOGY

Read more on page 84

E

EARTH   *ERTH*   *noun*

We live on planet Earth. It is the only planet that doesn't share a name with a Roman god. (For example, Mars is the god of war, and Jupiter is the god of the sea.) Earth's name describes the land on its surface. It means "dirt," "soil," or "ground," from a very early Proto-Indo-European root.

EASEL   *EE-zul*   *noun*

An easel is a wooden frame and stand used by artists to hold up their canvas while they paint. It comes from the Dutch *ezel*, which literally meant "donkey." The frame was named after a donkey because it holds your canvas up while you're painting, similar to the way a donkey can hold your things on its back.

EBULLIENT   *ee-BOO-lee-int*   *adjective*

To feel ebullient is to be so excited about something that you can't contain yourself. It's almost like a pot boiling so rapidly that it overflows! It comes from the Latin *ebullire*, meaning "to boil over." The Latin is formed from the prefix *ex-*, meaning "out," and *bullire*, meaning "to bubble."

ECCENTRIC   *ek-SENT-rik*   *adjective/noun*

The word "eccentric" describes someone who behaves in a nontraditional or whimsical way. But it was originally an astronomical term! Early astronomers believed that most planets orbited around Earth. (We now know that the planets in our solar system orbit around the sun.) These ancient astronomers called the planets that did not orbit Earth "eccentric." This comes from the Greek *ekkentros*, meaning "out of the center." Like these supposedly uncentered planets, an eccentric person might behave in a way that is unique or stands out.

ECLIPSE

ee-KLIPS   *noun*

A solar eclipse happens when the moon passes between Earth and the sun, blocking the sun from the Earth for a short period of time. A lunar eclipse happens when the Earth comes between the sun and the moon, leaving the moon in the Earth's shadow and making the moon appear darker for a short period of time. The word "eclipse" comes from the Greek *ekleipein*, which literally means "to leave out." We can take this to mean "fail to appear" or "to not appear in a usual place."

ECONOMY

uh-CON-uh-mee   *noun*

When it comes to a country's economy, we can think of it like a nation's wallet or bank account. It has to do with how the money goes in and out to support its citizens. But "economy" originally focused on something much smaller—the home. It comes from the Greek *oikonomia*, which means "household management." The meaning extended to larger-scale economies, because, in order to manage a home country well, you must manage your money well, too. The prefix *eco-* (or *oiko* in Greek) means "home" or "habitation." It also appears in words like "ecology," the study of natural habitats and the environment, and "ecosystem," the way animal and plant habitats support one another and thrive.

EGOCENTRIC

EE-go-SEN-trik   *adjective/noun*

The first part of this word is "ego," which is the Latin word for "I" or "the self." The second part, centric, comes from the Latin *centrum*, meaning "center." So, an egocentric person is literally "self-centered." They believe or act like they are at the center of everything.

ELECTRIC   uh-LEK-trik   *adjective*

The word "electric" was coined by the physicist William Gilbert in the 1600s from the Latin *electricus*, which literally means "resembling amber." Amber is hard, golden-colored, fossilized resin that comes from ancient, extinct trees. When you rub amber against certain substances, like wool or a cat's fur, it will generate static electricity.

ELF   *ELF*   *noun*

While the exact origin of this word is unknown, most etymologists believe that these mythical creatures get their name from the Germanic root *albho-,* meaning "white." While the earliest elves in folklore were small and mischievous, fairy stories influenced the idea of elegant, friendly elves—first in Edmund Spenser's *The Faerie Queene*, and later in J. R. R. Tolkien's *The Hobbit* and *The Lord of the Rings*.

EMBELLISH   em-BELL-ish   *verb*

Something that is embellished is decorated or ornamented. The word derives from the Old French *embellir*, meaning "to make beautiful," from the Latin base word *bellus*, or "beautiful."

EMERGE   ee-MERDJ   *verb*

To emerge from a place is to come out of it. When you get up in the morning, you emerge from your bedroom. This word comes from the Latin *emergere*, meaning "to bring out," "to rise," or "to come up." The Latin is made up of the prefix *ex-*, or "out," and *mergere*, meaning "to dip" or "sink." In a sense, emerging is to rise up out of something.

EMPATHY   EM-puh-thee   *noun*

"Empathy" is the ability to understand and share someone else's feelings. It comes from the Greek *empatheia*, which is made up of the prefix *em-*, meaning "in," and *pathos*, meaning "feeling." The Greek word was first translated into the German word *Einfühlung* by German philosophers before it was used in English.

EMPEROR
EM-pur-ur   noun

An emperor is the sole ruler of an empire, a collection of nations under one leader. The word comes from the Latin *imperare*, meaning "to command." Emperor penguins were given their royal name because they are the largest species of penguin.

ENCHANT
en-CHANT   verb

To enchant is to put a magical spell on someone or something. If you feel enchanted, you might be looking at something so amazing that you feel like it could be magic! It comes from the Old French *enchanter*, meaning "to bewitch," "to charm," or "to cast a spell." It was thought that some magical creatures could put spells on people by singing, which is why the original Latin *incantare* literally means "to sing into," from the prefix *in-*, meaning "into," and *cantare*, meaning "to sing." (*Incantare* is also the source of "incantation.")

ENEMY
EN-uh-mee   noun

Today, to "unfriend" someone is to remove them from your social media account. But an enemy was the original unfriend—literally. It comes from the Latin word *inimicus*, meaning someone who is an "unfriend," or someone whom you do not love. The Latin is made up of the prefix *in-* meaning "un" and *amicus*, meaning "friend."

ENERGETIC
EN-ur-JET-ik   adjective

If you're feeling energetic, you're full of energy. You're ready to run around or participate in fun activities. Both "energetic" and "energy" originally come from the Greek *energos*, meaning "active" or literally "at work." *Energos* is made up of the prefix *en-*, or "at," and *ergon*, meaning "work."

ENTHUSIASTIC en-THOO-zee-ass-tik adjective

If you're enthusiastic about something, you feel so excited about it that you can barely control your good emotions. In Ancient Greek, *enthousiastikos* was a word for someone who wasn't in control of their emotions because they were thought to be possessed by a god or goddess. The base word *entheos* is made up of *en-*, "in," and *theos*, "god," suggesting that an enthusiastic person has a god inside them.

ENTOMOLOGY
ENT-oh-mawl-oh-gee

noun

This word is often confused with "etymology," but while etymology is the study of words, entomology is the study of something else entirely—bugs. *Entomon* is Greek for "insect" and is made up of the prefix *en-*, meaning "in," and *temnein*, meaning "to cut." The "cutting" element is due to the way insects' bodies are segmented into three parts—head, thorax, and abdomen.

EPIDEMIC EP-i-DEM-ik adjective/noun

Today, this word refers to when a large group of people get really sick at the same time. But in the 1600s, it wasn't so sad. It just meant something happening to many people at once. It comes from the Greek *epidemia*, literally meaning "upon a community" or "among a group of people." The Greek word is made up of *epi*, meaning "among" or "upon," and *demos*, meaning "people" or "district."

EPISODE EP-i-sohd noun

An episode is usually a word for a single part of a long story, such as a TV series. In Ancient Greek plays, episodes were short scenes that divided up the main parts of the story. They usually included a chorus of singers who would sing about the different parts of the story. In Greek, the word was *epeisodion*, where *epi-* meant "in addition" and *eisodos* meant "an entrance." Over time, "episode" came to mean a part of any long story.

ERUPTION
ee-RUP-shun   *noun*

An eruption is when something bursts or explodes from below, like lava from a volcano. It comes from the Latin *erumpere*, which means "to break out" or "to burst forth," from the prefix *ex-*, or "out," and the base word *rumpere*, meaning "to break."

ETHEREAL
uh-THEER-ee-ull   *adjective*

The "ether" (Latin *aether*) is a term for the upper regions of Earth's atmosphere between the clouds and space. It is derived from the Greek *aithein*, meaning "to burn or shine." You might say something is "ethereal" if it is bright and airy like the ether. For the same reasons, "ether" was also the name of a clear, airy chemical used by nineteenth-century doctors to make patients drift into sleep.

EUCALYPTUS
YOO-ka-lip-tus   *noun*

Eucalyptus is an Australian species of evergreen tree known for its thick foliage. It creates shade for the animals and plants below, and it is koalas' favorite food! Eucalyptus is also used in many teas and herbal remedies. Its name, which literally means "well-covered," was coined in the 18th century by botanists who used the Greek components *eu* "well," and *kalyptos* "covered."

EUPHORIC
yoo-FOR-ik   *adjective*

To be euphoric is to be extremely happy. This word was originally a term doctors used for the feeling of being healthy and comfortable. It was adopted directly from Greek and is made up of the elements *eu*, meaning "well," and *pherein*, meaning "to carry."

EVALUATE   ee-VAL-yoo-ate   *verb*

To evaluate something is to decide on its quality or value. For example, you might evaluate someone's understanding of mathematics with a test or exam, which is sometimes called an "evaluation." If you inherited a gold necklace, you could take it to someone to evaluate how much it is worth. This word was adopted from the French *evaluer*, meaning "to find the value of." This word comes from the Latin *valere*, meaning "to be strong" or "to be of value." The "e" at the beginning comes from the Latin prefix *ex-*, meaning "out." So, to evaluate is to point out or show the value or strength of something.

EVOKE   ee-VOHK   *verb*

When you evoke something, you remind your listeners (or readers) of a familiar memory or a popular story. For example, if you mention a rabbit hole, you might evoke *Alice's Adventures in Wonderland* by Lewis Carroll, which begins with Alice falling down a hole after the white rabbit. "Evoke" comes from the Latin *evocare*, which means "to call out" or "to summon."

Example: The smell of apple pie evokes memories of Thanksgiving dinner at my grandmother's house.

EVOLUTION   EV-oh-LOO-shun   *noun*

Evolution is the process by which something changes over time. According to evolutionary theory, humans (*Homo sapiens*) evolved from apes, and birds evolved from dinosaurs. The word "evolve" comes from the Latin *evolvere*, meaning "to unroll or unfold." When you think of evolution, you can imagine a story that unfolds across time.

EXASPERATE   eg-ZAS-pur-ate   *verb*

Someone who is exasperated is frustrated or worn down. The Greek base word, *asper*, means "rough." Adding the prefix *ex-* intensifies the base word (or makes it stronger), suggesting the meaning "thoroughly roughened." In other words, they've gone through something or been "roughed up."

EXCITE   *ek-SIYT*   *verb*

When you're excited, you feel ready to get moving and take action! This word is derived from the Latin *exciere*, meaning "to call forth" or to set something in motion.

EXCLAIM   *eks-KLAYM*   *verb*

When you read aloud a sentence that ends in an exclamation point, you would probably raise your voice or even shout it. The origin of "exclaim" is the Latin *clamere*, meaning "to shout, cry, or call." It shares this source with the word "clamor," which means a loud, confused noise, like people shouting all at once. If you add the prefix *ex-*, meaning "out," this concept of shouting is intensified to "shout out."

EXPEDITION   *EKS-puh-DISH-un*   *noun*

An expedition is a journey to explore a new place. It originally described an army setting out on a mission, but its roots reveal much more than that. "Expedition" comes from the Latin *expedire*, which means "to prepare" or "to make ready" to go elsewhere. The Latin is made up of the prefix *ex-*, meaning "out," and *pedis*, meaning "a chain for the feet." In this sense, the word means to free yourself to venture somewhere new.

EXPLORE   *ek-SPLOR*   *verb*

The Latin *explorare* has the same meaning as our word does today—to investigate or search for something. Its literal meaning is "to cry out loudly" with *plorare* meaning "to weep" or "to cry." Some etymologists think that the meaning came from hunters who would search for animals and shout out loud to each other when they found one.

EXTRAVAGANT   *ek-STRAV-uh-gunt*   *adjective*

Someone who lives an extravagant lifestyle might indulge more than most people do. This word is derived from the Latin *extravagari*, meaning "to wander outside or beyond," formed of the base words *extra* "outside of" and *vagari*, meaning "to roam."

FOSSIL

Read more on page 92

F

FABLE   *FAY-bull*   *noun*

Fables are short stories that teach lessons. Aesop's fable "The Lion and the Mouse" teaches us to help others because they may one day be able to help us in return. Aesop was a Greek storyteller who passed his stories down by word of mouth. The word "fable" comes from the Latin *fabula*, meaning "that which is told." Someone who writes fables is called a "fabulist."

FALCON   *FAL-kun*   *noun*

"Falcon" derives from Latin *falx*, meaning "curved blade," much like their talons. Originally the word "falcon" referred only to female birds, while "tercel"—from the Latin *tertius*, meaning "third"—referred to males. Tercel was a clever name because male birds are one-third smaller than females.

FAMOUS   *FAY-muss*   *adjective*

A famous person is someone who everyone knows of and talks about—literally. It comes from the Latin *famosus*, meaning "frequently talked about," based on an earlier root meaning "to speak or tell."

FANFARE   *FAN-fair*   *noun*

"Fanfare," a flourishing sound from trumpets or bugles, was adopted from the French word *fanfare*, borrowed from the Arabic *farfar*, a word that imitated babbling speech. Similarly, the Spanish *fanfarron* meant someone who brags or boasts often. Today, fanfare also refers to the extra attention someone gets in the news, or anytime someone makes a big deal about a person or event.

Example: American gymnasts returned home to Washington, D.C., with great fanfare after they won the Olympic gold medal.

FASCINATE   *FASS-in-ate*   *verb*

If you're fascinated by something, you probably don't want to look away. It's almost like you've been enchanted or put under a magic spell. That's what the Romans might say, anyway, because "fascinate" comes from the Latin *fascinare*, meaning "to bewitch or enchant." It was thought that witches and serpents could cast a spell over people that forced them to look at the enchanter and do as they said.

FEDORA   *feh-DOR-uh*   *noun*

A fedora is a hat with a brim and a crease down the top that is often associated with detectives and adventurers like Indiana Jones. It was named after an 1889 play called *Fédora*. The main character of the play was a Russian princess named Fédora Romazov, and she was played by the actress Sarah Bernhardt, who was well-known for preferring to wear "men's" clothes. Bernhardt wore a brimmed hat like this during the play, and she became so popular for it that the hat was named after the character she played. The hat even became a symbol of the women's rights movement, which at the time involved fighting to get women the right to vote.

FERRET   *FAIR-itt*   *noun*

The name of these mischievous, long-bodied rodents comes from the Old French *furet*, which literally means "little thief." This is from the Latin *fur*, also meaning "thief."

FICTION   *FIK-shun*   *noun*

When authors write books about things that only happened in their imagination, we say those stories are "fiction." True accounts of real events and people are called "nonfiction." Have you ever made up a fictional story? It's almost like you're molding the characters and the world out of clay—and that's what the origin of this word means. It comes from the Latin *fictionem*, a word whose root means "to shape, pretend, or knead out of clay," from *fingere*, meaning "to form" or "to shape."

FIGMENT *FIG-ment* noun

A figment of your imagination is something that isn't really there but that you've created in your mind. This word comes from the Latin *fig-mentum*, meaning "creation" or "something formed."

FLAMINGO *fluh-MEEN-goh* noun

Flamingos are birds famous for their long legs and the bright pink hue of their feathers, which they get from eating brine shrimp and algae that contain a natural dye. Their name was adopted from the Portuguese and Spanish word *flamengo*, which literally means "flame-colored."

FLORAL *FLOH-rull* adjective

Flora was the Roman goddess of flowers. She gets her name from the Latin *florem*, the same source as the word "flower." Flora is the inspiration behind the words "florist" (someone who arranges flowers) and "floral," which refers to flowers' scent or flower-patterned designs.

FLUENT *FLOO-int* adjective

If you're fluent in a foreign language, you can speak it so well that it flows out of you just as easily as your first language. It comes from the Latin *fluere*, meaning "to flow."

FORTIFY *FORT-uh-fye* verb

Fortify means "to make strong." The Latin *fortis*, meaning "strong," is the origin of many words that mean "strong" in English, too. For example, a fortress is a strong place that can be defended from enemies. If you comfort someone, you make them stronger by being together with them.

FOSSIL

FAW-sill

noun

Fossils are buried creatures that died long ago and were preserved by rock and earth. Where are fossils found? In the ground, of course! That's why this word comes from the Latin *fossilis*, meaning something "dug up." The English word "fossil" was first recorded in the 1600s. Yet, for almost a century later it was used to refer to anything that had been dug up from the ground, not just prehistoric bones and petrified trees.

FRAGILE

FRADJ-ull　　　*adjective*

Something that is fragile, like a glass vase, might shatter if you knocked it to the ground. It comes from the Latin *fragilis*, meaning "easily broken." It shares the same root, meaning "break," with the words "fragment," "fracture," and "fraction."

FRENZY

FREN-zee　　　*noun*

To be in a frenzy is to be extremely upset, worried, or excited. It is related to the less common word "frenetic," which comes from the Greek phrase *phrenitis nosos*. This was a medical term meaning "an inflammation of the brain" that was thought to cause temporary insanity! The base word *phren* meant "mind" or "reason," and *nosos* meant "disease" or "inflammation."

FRICTION

FRIK-shun　　　*noun*

When one object rubs against another or is dragged across a surface, it creates friction, or resistance. The word comes from the Latin *fricare*, meaning "to rub." While it is a scientific term, it can also be used to describe tension between people or groups of people.

Example: There was friction between the siblings who both wanted the last cupcake.

FRIEND *FREND* *noun*

This word is one of the English language's oldest pals. It's been around for well over 1,000 years—maybe even 5,000! While its spelling has changed from *freond* in Old English to "friend" in Modern English, its meaning has remained true. It comes from a Proto-Indo-European root meaning "love."

FROLIC *FRAW-lik* *verb*

To frolic means to have fun and to playfully bounce around. It comes from the Middle Dutch word *vrolyc*, meaning "happy." The earlier root, *preu-*, means "to hop." It's also the source of "frog," which gives "frolic" the sense of "jumping for joy."

FUNDAMENTAL *FUN-duh-MENT-ul* *adjective*

Something fundamental is the most basic part of something larger. For example, fundamental math skills would be addition and subtraction, and fundamental reading skills would include learning the alphabet. This word is related to and comes from the same source as the word "foundation." When you build a house, you start by making the ground under it strong and flat. This ground is called the "foundation," and it helps you build the rest of the house. Both "fundamental" and "foundation" come from the Latin *fundare*, meaning "to lay a bottom."

FUNKY *FUN-kee* *adjective*

This word comes from French and Latin words for "smoke"—as in smoked cheese! "Funky" has meant a lot of different things over time. It's been used to describe a spark, a state of fear, a bad mood, and a cheesy or unpleasant odor.

Example: His room smelled funky after he left his dirty gym socks on the floor.

GNOME

Read more on page 97

G

GALAXY   *GAL-ak-see*   *noun*

A galaxy is a collection of billions of stars held together by gravity. Earth's solar system is part of the Milky Way galaxy, which you can see on clear, dark nights. It almost looks like someone splashed milk across the night sky! Before powerful telescopes showed us that there are trillions of galaxies in the universe, the Milky Way was the only galaxy humans knew about. That's why the word "galaxy" comes from the Greek word for the Milky Way, *galaxias kyklos*, meaning "milky circle." *Galaxias* originally comes from the Greek *gala*, meaning "milk," and *kyklos* meant "circle" or "wheel."

GAMBIT   *GAM-bit*   *noun*

Making a risky but clever decision is called a gambit. If you're playing a board game, you might make a clever move to get an advantage over the person you're playing against. It comes from the Italian *gambetto*, the name of a wrestling trick that involves tripping up an opponent, from the word *gamba*, or "leg."

Example: I thought I was winning at checkers when I took one of my sister's pieces. It turned out to be a gambit—she took three of my pieces in a row!

GAME   *GAYM*   *noun*

Most games aren't much fun if they're played without friends. In Old English, the word for "game" is *gamen*, which comes from a Proto-Germanic root meaning "people together."

GENDER   *JEN-dur*   noun

Gender and sex are often confused. A person's "sex" is biological and defined at birth. But "gender" refers to an individual, social, and cultural expression of who you are. In many societies, gender is very closely tied to sex, but this is evolving. Gender exists on a spectrum, and so do the pronouns that go with it. You might identify as a girl with the pronouns she/her, as a boy with the pronouns he/him, or somewhere unique with the pronouns they/them. Some people prefer other pronouns, too. The word "gender" comes from the Latin *genos*, meaning "kind"—as in some kind of person.

GENETIC   *juh-NET-ik*   adjective

A gene is a unit of hereditary material that is passed down from parents to their babies. Genetic traits appear as the features you're born with like eye color, hair color, and blood type. It comes from the Greek *genesis*, meaning "origin."

GEYSER   *GUY-zer*   noun

A geyser is a spring or water source that is heated by the earth and sometimes shoots hot steam high into the air. The English word "geyser" was adopted from the Icelandic *Geysir*, meaning "the gusher."

GHOST   *GOHST*   noun

In scary stories and legends, a ghost is the spirit of a person who has passed away. If you were to see a ghost, you might gasp or breathe rapidly in fear. The word comes from the Old English *gast*, which was sometimes used to mean "breath."

GIRAFFE   *jeer-AFF*   noun

The name for this long-necked animal was borrowed from the Italian *giraffa* in the 1590s. It originally comes from the animals' Arabic name, *zarafa*. Before the 1590s, the English word for a giraffe was *camelopard*, or camel-leopard, thanks to its camel-like body and leopard-like spots.

GLUTTONY *GLUT-ton-nee* noun

Gluttony is the act of eating and drinking too much. A person who is a glutton would eat greedily at the dinner table and not leave enough for everyone else! This word is related to the Latin *gluttire*, meaning "to swallow," and *gula*, meaning "throat."

GNOME

NOHM

noun

When you picture a gnome, you probably imagine a little bearded person with a pointed hat. But gnomes have been imagined differently by different cultures and storytellers. Sometimes they appear as tiny people who look like they're made of wood. In other stories, they look more like magical fairies. The one thing that's stayed consistent is that people believe they live in tree trunks or dwell in holes in the ground. This is most likely why their name comes from a Greek source meaning "earth-dweller."

GOBLET *GOB-let* noun

A goblet is a type of cup that was common in the Middle Ages. It gets its name from *gob*, an early English word for "mouth" or "mouthful." You might also recognize it in the words "gobble" and "gobstopper."

GOLD *GOHLD* noun

Gold is one of the most expensive metals in the world because it can easily be shaped into jewelry or wires. It's very durable, and it conducts electricity. Of course, it's also prized because of its bright color, which is why its name comes from a Proto-Indo-European root meaning "to shine." The words "glitter" and "glow" also share the same root.

GOPHER   *GO-fer*   *noun*

Gophers are a type of rodent known for digging complex underground tunnels to build their home. Etymologists believe that gophers get their name from the Louisiana French word *gaufre*, which means "honeycomb" or "waffle," because of the similarity between these foods and the interlocking shape of gopher tunnels.

GORGEOUS   *GOR-jyuss*   *adjective*

Someone or something who is gorgeous is extremely attractive. In Middle French, its source word *gorgias* means "elegant" or "fashionable." This word most likely comes from the Old French *gorge*, meaning "throat" because, at the time, long and graceful necks were considered attractive, especially with expensive necklaces that could show them off.

GRADUATE   *GRAD-yoo-et*   *noun/verb*

When you graduate from middle school to high school, you're taking a step up in your education. It comes from the Latin *gradus*, a word for an actual step on a staircase or ladder.

GRAMMAR   *GRAM-mer*   *noun*

Grammar is a set of rules for forming correct phrases and sentences. It comes from the Latin *gramma*, which means "letter," but its definition was once much broader. "Grammar" could once refer to any type of learning or education, rather than just lessons related to words and letters. It could even mean the practice of learning or studying different types of spells and incantations.

GRATITUDE   *GRAT-ih-tood*   *noun*

Gratitude is the state of being grateful or thankful for something. You can express gratitude for a gift you received, the love of your parents, or a healthy meal. You can feel gratitude for almost anything that makes you happy or feel at ease. The word comes from the Latin *gratus*, meaning "pleasing."

GREGARIOUS   greh-GAIR-ee-us   *adjective*

A gregarious person is someone who is very social. They might enjoy big parties or being in large crowds. Back in the 1600s, it was used to describe animals that live in flocks, like sheep and goats. It comes from the Latin *grex*, meaning "flock or herd." *Grex* is also the origin of the modern word "congregate," meaning "to gather together."

GRIM   *GRIM*   *adjective*

If your facial expression is grim, you're probably not very happy. After all, a grim situation is very serious and dangerous. It comes from a Proto-Germanic root meaning "fierce" or "angry." The root word may have even been meant to imitate the sound of rolling thunder.

GRINCH   *GRINCH*   *noun*

The word "grinch" was popularized by Dr. Seuss in his 1957 book *How the Grinch Stole Christmas!* But Dr. Seuss was not the first author to use it. Rudyard Kipling, the author of *The Jungle Book*, most likely invented this word and used it as an adjective, *grinching*, meaning "a harsh grating noise," in a poem in 1892.

GRUMPY   *GRUM-pee*   *adjective*

To be grumpy means to be in a bad mood. This is probably related to the Danish word *grum*, meaning "cruel" or "grumble." When it first appeared in English, it was used as the full phrase "humps and grumps," describing someone talking sourly or moodily. At this time, it was said someone "had a case of the grumps."

GUEST   *GEST*   *noun*

This word, spelled *gæst* or *giest* in Old English, originally meant "stranger." The rules of hospitality at the time said that any visitor to your house, even an unexpected stranger, should be welcomed as a guest and provided with food and shelter.

HIPPOPOTAMUS

Read more on page 105

H

HABITAT *HAB-eh-tat* noun
A habitat is the natural area where animals (including humans) live. It comes from the Latin *habitare*, meaning "to live in."

HALLUCINATE *huh-LOO-sin-ate* verb
To hallucinate is to see, hear, smell, taste, or feel something that isn't truly there. It comes from the Latin *alucinari*, meaning "to wander (in the mind)" or "to dream."

HALO *HAY-loh* noun
A halo is commonly seen in religious illustrations and artwork, especially around the head of a figure such as the Virgin Mary or an angel. It comes from the Greek *halos*, meaning the circle or disk of light coming from the sun and moon.

HANGNAIL *HANG-nale* noun
You might think that "hangnail" has an obvious etymology, from "hang" and "nail." But it's actually from the Middle English *angnail*, meaning "a corn or knot on the foot." Its literal translation is "painful spike" from the Proto-Indo-European *angh-*, meaning "painful," and the Old English *nægl*, meaning "iron spike or nail." The idea was that a hard corn in your foot is rather like standing on the head of an iron nail or spike. *Angh-* is also the root of "anger," "anxious," and "anguish."

HAPPY *HAP-ee* adjective
If something good happened to you, you'd probably be happy. The words "happen" and "happy" come from the Old Norse *happ*, meaning "luck" or "chance." To be happy is to feel like you have good luck or good things are happening to you.

HARBOR
HAR-ber   noun

This word usually refers to a port along a coastline where boats can be stored. It can also mean a safe place or shelter for people. It comes from the Middle English word *herberwe*, meaning "army shelter."

HARVEST
HAR-vist   noun/verb

To harvest crops means to pick or collect them so that you can store them for winter or sell them. Harvest, or *hærfest*, was the Old English name for the autumn season, when many kinds of crops are ripe. The word comes from a Proto-Indo-European root meaning "to gather or pluck."

HAZARD
HAZZ-urd   noun

This word, meaning something dangerous or risky, is the name of a 14th-century dice game that was played in France. Most etymologists believe that the word "hazard" originally comes from *al-zahr*, the Arabic word for dice.

HEIST
HIYST   noun

A heist is a criminal's plan to steal something, usually a lot of money or something large. These attempts are often the subject of movies and TV shows. The word is probably a variation of "hoist," meaning "to lift something heavy," because "lift" is a slang word for the act of theft.

Example: The thieves planned an elaborate heist to steal artwork from the museum.

HELICOPTER
HEL-lih-copp-tur   noun

Helicopters are aircraft that use spinning propellers to lift themselves into the air. Some early helicopters had spiral-shaped wings. The word is a combination of the Greek *helix*, meaning "spiral," and *pteron*, meaning "wing."

HEMISPHERE   *HEM-iss-feer*   *noun*

The equator is an imaginary line around the middle of the Earth that divides the globe into two equal parts or hemispheres, the northern hemisphere and the southern hemisphere. But what's a hemisphere? Let's break it down: A sphere is an object shaped like a ball. The word "sphere" comes from the Greek *sphaira*, meaning "ball" or "globe." When you add the Greek prefix *hemi-*, meaning "half," to "sphere," the prefix cuts the ball or globe in half. So, a hemisphere is a half of a ball, or half of the globe.

HERO   *HEE-roh*   *noun*

In Greek, the word *heros* means "demi-god," or someone whose parents were one part god or goddess and one part human. For example, the famous warrior Achilles, who fought and died during the Trojan War, was said to be the son of a human and the water goddess Thetis. In mythology, heroes had special abilities and important destinies, just like the heroes of the stories we read today (even if they aren't the children of gods and goddesses).

HESITATE   *HEZ-uh-tate*   *verb*

When you're about to do something scary or difficult, it's normal to hesitate, or to wait a moment before starting. To hesitate is to give something a second thought. It comes from the Latin *haesitare*, meaning "to stick" or to be stuck in one place.

HIATUS   *hiy-ATE-us*   *noun*

To go on a hiatus means to take a break. It was borrowed from a Latin word with the same spelling, meaning "opening or gap." It shares a Proto-Indo-European root with the words "chaos," "chasm," "gasp," and "yawn." All of these words refer to something wide, open, or deep.

HICCUP   *HIK-up*   *noun/verb*

If you eat or drink too quickly, you might get the hiccups. This word has been spelled in a variety of ways throughout history, including *hickop, hicket,* and *hyckock.* Regardless of the spelling, the word is meant to imitate the sound you make when you hiccup. In Old English, hiccups were known as *ælfsogoða,* meaning "elf pains," because hiccups were thought to be caused by elves.

HIERARCHY   *HIY-ur-ark-ee*   *noun*

A hierarchy is a ranking of things from most important to least important. Think about the rankings on a ship: The captain is the most important in the hierarchy, the first mate ranks just below the captain, and the other sailors are below the first mate. This word originally comes from the Greek *hieros*, meaning "sacred," and *arkhein*, meaning "to lead" or "to rule."

HIEROGLYPHICS   *HIY-roh-gliff-iks*   *noun*

Ancient Egyptians used a writing system made of symbolic pictures and alphabetic elements called hieroglyphics or heiroglyphs. It originally comes from the Greek *hieros,* meaning "sacred," and *glyphe*, meaning "carving." The Greek was a translation of the Egyptian word for the symbols, which meant "god's words."

HIPPOCAMPUS   *HIP-poh-kam-pus*   *noun*

The hippocampus is a part of the brain that helps control emotion, memory, and the nervous system. It is shaped almost exactly like a seahorse, which is where it gets its name. The Latin word *hippocampus* was a word for a seahorse that literally means "horselike sea monster."

HIPPOPOTAMUS
HIP-oh-pott-eh-muss

noun

Despite their huge size, these mammals are very good swimmers and spend most of their time in African rivers. Their name is Greek for "river horse," a combination of *hippos*, meaning "horse," and *potamos*, meaning "river" or "rushing water."

HORIZON   *HOR-iy-zun*   *noun*

The horizon is the line in the far distance where it looks like the sky meets the earth. A horizontal line goes side to side, like the horizon, versus a vertical line that goes up and down. The Greek *horizein* means "divide" or "separate." In Old English, the word was *eaggemearc*, which meant "eye-mark" because the horizon is as far as you can see across the land.

HORROR   *HOR-orr*   *noun*

When you watch a horror movie, you might get so scared that you start shaking. You might even feel the tiny hairs on your neck and arms stand up, or bristle. The word "horror" comes from that feeling. The Latin word *horrere* means "to shudder" or "to bristle with fear."

HUMBLE   *HUM-bull*   *adjective*

This word's source is the Latin *humus*, meaning "earth," because to be humble is not to elevate yourself but be modest and unprideful. It shares its root with "humiliate," which suggests bringing someone (maybe even yourself) back to earth, keeping you humble.

Example: Even though she got an "A" on her paper, she was humble about it. She didn't brag when she saw that most of her classmates didn't pass.

HUMOR
HYOO-mer   noun

"Humor" refers to something that is funny. The word comes from the Latin *umor*, meaning "bodily fluid," from the Latin base word *umere*, meaning "be wet, moist." If that doesn't sound that funny, that's because until the 1680s, the word "humor" had nothing to do with comedy. Instead, it referred to the liquids in your body that were thought to control your mood and emotions. Pretty funny, right? Now we know that liquids don't really have anything to do with our moods. Over time, the word "humor" started to mostly mean "a good mood" because these humors changed your mood. Today, it means anything that puts you in a good mood by making you laugh.

HUSKY
HUSS-key   noun

With their warm fur and padded feet, husky dogs are well suited to running in the snow, often pulling sleds in teams. The name of this hardy dog breed is a shortening of the Canadian English *Ehuskemay*, another way to spell "Eskimo." Eskimo is a name that Algonquian Native Americans and early American explorers used for people who lived in the Arctic region. However, most people from these northern cultures call themselves "Inuit" and usually prefer to be called by that name.

HYBRID
HIY-bred   adjective/noun

A hybrid, or *hybrida* in Latin, refers to any sort of mixing of two elements or qualities. For example, a hybrid car combines electricity and fuel to power it. If you get a vanilla and chocolate swirl, that's a hybrid ice cream cone. The Latin word once had a very specific meaning: a type of pig that resulted when a male wild boar mated with a tame female pig.

ROOT SPOTLIGHT: *HYDR-*

Review the definitions and etymologies of these terms that include the Greek root *hydr-* or *hydro-*.

- **HYDRATE:** to have enough water to drink, from the Greek *hydr-*, meaning "water."

- **HYDRA:** a legendary monster with many heads, from the Greek *hydor*, meaning "water," because it was said to live in the sea.

- **FIRE HYDRANT:** a public fixture beside a street that allows quick access to water in case of a fire, from *hydor* + the ending *-ant*, which is often used for tools and devices.

- **HYDRAULIC POWER:** power generated by the movement of water, from *hydor* + *aulos*, meaning "musical instrument" or "pipe." A *hydraulikos organon* was a musical instrument that used moving water to make sound. The instrument's name inspired machines that use water to make power.

- **HYDROGEN:** a gaseous element, from *hydor* "water" + the French ending *-gène*, meaning "producing." It means "water-producing" because hydrogen gas combines with oxygen to form water molecules (H_2O).

All of these words relate to water and come from the Greek *hydor*. Although Hydra—the great sea monster—had been part of folklore for centuries, this root showed up in English more often after the 1600s, when hydraulic power became more common and hydrogen was discovered and named.

Still thirsty? Go have a glass of water to stay hydrated!

HYPERBOLE · hiy-PER-boh-lee · noun

When you say "My homework will take forever!" or "My backpack weighs a ton!" you are using hyperbole, or an extreme exaggeration. After all, your homework will probably only take an hour, and your backpack probably only weighs a few pounds. "Hyperbole" was adopted directly from the Greek *hyperbole*, meaning "a throwing beyond." It is made up of the elements *hyper-*, meaning "beyond" or "over," and *bole*, meaning "a throwing."

HYPNOTIZE · HIP-noh-tyze · verb

"You are getting very sleepy . . ." To hypnotize someone is to put them in a trancelike or sleeplike state. Hypnosis is often used in magic shows, but this type of hypnosis is usually a trick. In real hypnosis, you probably won't be clucking like a chicken. Instead, a doctor or therapist might use it to make someone relax, concentrate very deeply, and focus on their inner thoughts. This "trancelike" meaning didn't become common until the mid-1800s. Before that, "hypnotic" described a type of medicine that makes you sleepy. It comes from the Greek *hypnotikos*, meaning "sleepy," from the base word *hypnos*, or "sleep."

HYPOTHESIS · hiy-PAW-thuh-sis · noun

When you perform a science experiment, you start by making a hypothesis, or an educated guess about what will happen at the end of the experiment. In Greek, *hypothesis* meant "foundation" or "base," or literally "a placing under." It is made up of the parts *hypo-*, meaning "under," and *thesis*, meaning "a placing." In science, the purpose of your whole experiment is to find out whether the hypothesis is true or not.

INCOGNITO

Read more on page 113

I

IDEA   *iy-DEE-uh*   *noun*

This word was borrowed from the Greek *idea*, meaning "to see," thanks to the philosopher Plato. The way Plato saw it, the real world—or the physical things we can perceive with our five senses—wasn't as real as our ideas, our thoughts, and the things we imagine. For Plato, we see through the lens of our ideas.

IDENTITY   *iy-DEN-tih-tee*   *noun*

Your identity is, very basically, what and who you are. It can also describe the way you understand yourself and the way the world sees you. The word comes from the Latin *idem*, meaning "the same."

IGLOO   *IG-loo*   *noun*

An igloo is a dome-shaped structure made of ice that provides warmth and shelter in frozen Arctic climates. It comes from a word meaning "house" in the language of the Inuit people who live in the Arctic.

IGNEOUS   *IG-nee-us*   *adjective*

Igneous rocks are formed by the fiery heat of underground volcanoes. The word comes from the Latin *ignis*, meaning "fire." The word "ignite" has the same origin.

IGNORE   *IG-nor*   *verb*

If you're ignoring someone, you are pretending they are not there. Originally, this word had a slightly different meaning in English. It meant that you were not aware of something, or that you didn't know it, instead of intentionally not paying attention to it. That is why the similar word "ignorant" describes someone who is not knowledgeable or is not aware of something. Both are formed by the prefix *in-*, meaning "the opposite of," and *gnarus*, meaning "aware."

ILLUMINATE   uh-LOO-min-ate   verb

When you shine a light on something, you illuminate it. This is physical—
you can illuminate a dark space by shining a light in that direction. It
is also a metaphor—you illuminate an idea or new way of thinking by
gaining information where you were previously "in the dark." Illuminate
comes from the Latin *illuminare*, meaning "to throw into light," from the
prefix *in-*, meaning "on," and *lumen*, meaning "light."

*Example: When the archaeologists entered the ancient tomb, the torchlight illumi-
nated piles of riches around the sarcophagus.*

ILLUSION   uh-LOO-zhun   noun

When a magician seems to make a person disappear, she is performing
an illusion, or something that tricks your eyes. The word "illusion" originally meant "mockery" or "scorning," from the Latin *illudere*, meaning
"to mock" or "to play with." This is because an illusionist plays with what
you think you see.

IMAGINE   ih-MAJ-inn   verb

"Imagine" comes from the Latin *imaginari*, meaning "to form a mental
picture." *Imaginari* is originally from the Latin *imitari,* which means to
"copy" or "imitate." This is because when you imagine something, you
create a picture or copy of it in your mind.

IMMEDIATE   im-MEED-ee-it   adjective

Something immediate is about to happen right now, without any delay.
It comes from the Latin *immediatus*, meaning "without anything in
between," and is formed by the prefix *im-* ("not, opposite of") and
mediatus ("in the middle").

IMMERSE   *IM-urss*   *verb*

To be immersed in something is to be completely covered by it. When you go swimming, you immerse yourself in water. When you enjoy a book so much that you feel you've been transported into the world of the characters, you're immersed in the story. It comes from the Latin *immergere*, meaning "to plunge in."

IMMIGRANT   *IM-mig-runtt*   *noun*

An immigrant is someone who moves to a different country from the one they were born in. The base of this word is "migrate," which is often used to describe the flight of birds that travel south for the cold winter months. Both come from the Latin *migrare*, meaning "to move from one place to another."

IMPRESS   *im-PRESS*   *verb*

To impress someone is to do something that makes them remember you, especially in a positive way. It's almost as if your meaningful action leaves a permanent stamp in their memory—and that's what the word's etymology means. It comes from the Latin *imprimere*, meaning "to stamp" or "to press into," from the prefix *in-*, meaning "on" or "in," and *premere*, meaning "to press."

IMPROVISE   *IM-proh-vyz*   *verb*

Have you ever forgotten the words to a song you're singing and then sing different words instead? You improvised! To improvise is to do something without preparing for it. This word comes from the Latin *improvisus*, meaning "unexpected," from the prefix *in-*, meaning "not" or "opposite of," and *provisus*, meaning "provided" or "foreseen."

INCOGNITO

IN-cog-nee-toh

adjective

To be incognito means to be in disguise or to conceal your identity. For example, a spy might go incognito, or undercover in a disguise, in order to learn more about an enemy. It comes from the Latin *incognitus*, meaning "unknown."

INDEPENDENT   *IN-dih-pen-dint*   *adjective*

Imagine if you nearly fell from a ledge, and the only thing preventing you from falling was the fact that you were holding on to your friend's hand. Your life would depend upon your friend's grip. This is the literal sense of the word "dependent." The word comes from the Latin *dependere,* meaning "to hang down from." The base word *pendere* means "to hang" or "weigh," and if you add the prefix *in-*, meaning "opposite of," you get "independent." To do something independently is to do it without the hand (or help) of someone else.

Example: For our group science project, we had to turn in one poster made by the whole group, but each person also had to write an independent essay about what they had learned.

INDIGO   *IN-duh-goh*   *adjective*

Indigo is a rich blue and purple color that is one of the seven light refractions that appears in the rainbow. The word comes from the Spanish *indico,* the name of a vivid blue dye that's used for inks and clothing. Its original source is the Greek *indikon,* literally meaning "Indian substance" but used specifically for this type of blue dye, which was first made from plants in India.

INDUSTRY   *IN-duh-stree*   *noun*

Today we think of industry in connection with business and advanced technology. But according to its origin, everything you need to create the industry of the future is within you. In English, it first meant "cleverness" or "skillfulness." It originally comes from the Latin *indu*, meaning "within," and *struere*, "to build."

INFAMOUS   *IN-fuh-muss*   *adjective*

This word originally meant someone who was not famous at all, but over time it evolved to mean someone who was famous for a poor reputation, such as committing crimes or other misdeeds. It comes from Latin and is formed of the prefix *in-*, meaning "not," and *famosus*, meaning "celebrated." A famous person is celebrated, while an infamous person is feared for the bad things they do.

INFINITY   *in-FIN-uh-tee*   *noun*

Infinity is a number that is so large that it is beyond counting because it goes on forever. Something that is infinite also has no limits. It comes from the Latin *in-*, meaning "not," and *finis*, meaning "end."

INNOCENT   *IN-oh-sent*   *adjective*

An innocent person isn't guilty of any crimes or wrongdoing. This word comes from the Latin *innocentem*, which has the same meaning. Breaking it down, it is made up of the prefix *in-*, meaning "not," and *nocere*, meaning "to harm." So, someone who is innocent does no harm.

INNOVATION   *IN-uh-VAY-shun*   *noun*

An innovation is a new thing or idea, and an innovator is someone who invents new things or comes up with new ideas. It comes from the Latin *innovare*, meaning "to renew" or "to change," combining the prefix *in*, or "into," and *novus*, meaning "new." These elements reflect the fact that innovations in art, science, and technology allow us to create new things, advance into new territory, and change the world.

PLAYING WITH PREFIXES: *IN-*

The prefix *in-* has many meanings. In some cases, like **infuriate**, it can be used to make a word stronger. In this example, *in-* is added to 'fury" to show that someone is extra angry. It can also be added to show that it is directed *into* something or someone, as in **invade** (to force one's way *into* someone's space), **intimidate** (to make someone feel timid *inside*), or **inquire** (to dive *into* a topic by asking questions about it).

In many cases, however, this prefix means "not," or "the opposite of," and it can be used to turn words into their own opposites. For example,

- Something that is **infinite** is not finite, meaning it has no end and goes on forever, from the Latin *finis*, or "end."

- A meeting or event that is **inconvenient** is not convenient, meaning it doesn't fit in well with your schedule, from the Latin *convenire*, "to meet together" or "to be suitable."

- Hunger that is **insatiable** cannot be satiated or satisfied, meaning you are endlessly hungry no matter how much you eat, originally from the Latin *satiare* "to satisfy."

Think about these words that become their own opposites when you add the prefix *in-*:

JUSTICE   **FORMAL**   **DIRECT**   **ATTENTIVE**

How does the meaning of each one change?

ANSWER KEY

injustice = something that is not just or not fair

informal = not formal, casual

indirect = not direct, not straight

inattentive = not paying attention

INQUISITIVE   *in-KWIZ-uh-tiv*   *adjective*

To be inquisitive is to be curious and ask many questions about a topic. It comes from the Medieval Latin *inquerere*, meaning "to seek into." This is made up of the prefix *in-* and the base word *quaerere*, meaning "to ask" or "to seek."

INSPIRE   *in-SPY-ur*   *verb*

When something inspires you, it makes you want to create something new or take on a new challenge. It comes from the Latin *inspirare*, which means "to breathe into." In Ancient Greece, people believed that prophets, called oracles, could understand the words of the gods. These gods would whisper or breathe their words into the prophets, and the prophets were said to be "inspired."

INTELLIGENCE   *in-TELL-ij-enss*   *noun*

Intelligence is the ability to use the knowledge you have. To use your intelligence is to apply your own thinking to work through a situation. It comes from the Latin *intelligere*, meaning "to understand." It is formed by the elements *inter*, or "between," and *legere*, meaning "to choose" or "to read." In this sense, the word literally means to read between the lines or understand things that aren't easy to see.

INTEREST   *IN-tur-est*   *noun*

Which school subject do you think is the most interesting? When you study that subject, you probably feel as if you want to keep learning about it more than any other subject. In Latin, the word *interest* meant "to be between or among," from the prefix *inter-*, meaning "between," and *esse*, meaning "to be." When you are interested in something, you feel as if you can fully immerse yourself in the subject or commit your mind to it.

INTERRUPT   IN-tur-upt   verb

To interrupt someone is to talk over them while they're talking, or to stop them while they're doing something else. This word comes from the Latin *interrumpere*, meaning "to break apart" or "to break through." It is made up of the Latin elements *inter*, "between," and *rumpere*, "to break."

INTROVERT   INT-row-vert   noun

An introvert is a person who would probably rather stay at home or be alone instead of going to a large party. This word is a combination of the Latin *intro*, meaning "inward," and *vertere*, meaning "to turn." So, if an introvert is someone who prefers to stay in, or focus inward on their own thoughts, can you guess what an extrovert is? The Latin *extra* means "outside," so an extrovert is someone who "turns outward," or likes to spend time out and about with many people. Both introverts and extroverts can be great friends and add much to the world!

INTRUDE   in-TROOD   verb

Do you have a sibling who loves to barge into your room all the time? To intrude is to enter or come close without someone's permission. It comes from the Latin *intrudere*, meaning "to force in," from the prefix *in-*, meaning "in," and *trudere*, meaning "to push."

ISOLATE   IY-soh-late   verb

To be isolated is to be alone or made to feel lonely, just like an island by itself in the ocean. The word comes from the Latin *insulatus*, meaning "made into an island." The base word *insula* means "island."

JEWEL

Read more on page 122

J

JABBER   *JAB-ber*   *verb*

Jabber means to talk very fast in a way that can be hard to hear or understand. "Jabber" is from the Old English *jablen*. (Other Old English variations included *javeren*, *jaberen*, and *jawin*.) Its use gave rise to "jibber-jabber." This then turned into "gibberish," which means senseless language.

JACK-O'-LANTERN *JAK-oh-LAN-turn*   *noun*

In the 1600s, "Jack-o'-lantern" was a word for a person who kept watch over a village at night while carrying a lantern. It literally means "Jack with the lantern." People back then used the name "Jack" because it was a very common name during that time period. (This is similar to how we use the phrase "average Joe" today.) It was also a word for a will-o'-the-wisp, which is a ghostly light that travelers on the road claimed to see on dark nights. It wasn't until 200 years later that people began to use it as a name for a festive Halloween pumpkin.

JACKAL   *JAK-uhl*   *noun*

A jackal is a type of canine, or dog, similar to a coyote that lives on most continents. Its name came to English from the French name for the animal, *chacal*, but originally comes from the Sanskrit (the language of Ancient India) *srgalah*, meaning "the howler."

JACKET   *JAK-it*   *noun*

This type of clothing has changed in appearance over the centuries. It was first a type of clothing specifically for men. It's probably called a "jacket" from the name Jacque, the French version of Jack. It could also be from the name of a *jaque de mailles*, or a coat of mail armor originally from the Arabic word *shakk*, which means "breastplate."

JADE   *JAYD*   *noun*

Jade is a type of precious gemstone and also the name of the stone's shade of green. Its name comes from the Spanish name for it, *piedra de la ijada*, meaning "stone of pain in the side." The stone was thought to cure these pains.

JAGUAR   *JAG-warr*   *noun*

Jaguars are spotted wild cats that are native to the Americas. Their name comes from the Tupi (Brazilian) word *jaguara*, which was probably a word for any large predator but became more specific over time.

JANITOR   *JAN-uh-ter*   *noun*

Today, a janitor is someone whose job is to clean and maintain schools, hospitals, offices, and other buildings. It comes from the Latin *ianitor*, meaning "doorkeeper." The word *ianus*, meaning "gate" or "passage-way," was also the name of the two-faced Roman god (called Janus in English) known for his association to beginnings and endings. The month January is named after Janus because he represents the end of one year and the beginning of the new year.

JARGON   *JAR-gun*   *noun*

Jargon is a name for the kinds of technical terms used by people in a particular profession. For example, a lawyer might talk about her work using legal jargon, or a doctor might use medical jargon. It originally meant "unintelligible talk" or "gibberish." It comes from the Old French *jargon*, meaning "a chattering," like chattering birds. This word's modern meaning was a way to poke fun at people who use technical words too much because that kind of language makes no sense to people outside of their jobs or hobbies.

JAZZ   *JAZZ*   *noun*

Jazz music was first played in New Orleans in the late 1800s. It comes from the American slang word *jasm*, which meant "energy" or "spirit."

JEALOUS   *JELL-uss*   *adjective*

To feel jealous is to want what someone else has or to fear someone will take away what's yours. This word is a variation of "zealous," which means "overenthusiastic" or "overly passionate" and comes from the Greek *zelos*. To be zealous, in ancient times, was considered a good thing because it had a milder definition and meant to simply care about someone or something very much. "Jealous" came about when the word evolved into the Old French *jalos*, adding a sense of intensity and envy to the word.

Example: I felt jealous when my best friend started hanging out with his soccer team on Fridays instead of playing video games at my house.

JEOPARDY   *JEP-arr-dee*   *noun*

Jeopardy, which means danger or risk, comes from the Old French *jeu parti*, meaning "a divided game." *Jeopardy!* is also a television game show. Merv Griffin, who created the game show, based it on a concept made by his wife, Julann Wright. It was first titled *What's the Question?* but changed after a network executive said, "It doesn't have enough jeopardies."

JESTER   *JESS-tur*   *noun*

Most people associate jesters with their colorful costumes, belled hats, and comedic performances. But in the medieval era, jesters weren't necessarily expected to tell jokes. Instead, they were expected to recite exciting tales. A "jest" (or *geste*) was a narrative or story of great deeds, and *gesten* was to recite one of these stories. These words all come from the Latin *gesta*, meaning "deeds" or what we might call "adventures."

JEWEL

JOOWL

noun

A jewel is a beautiful cut gemstone that you might see in a necklace or a ring. This word shares the same etymological source as the word "joke," the Latin *iocus* or *jocus*, because both are thought to cause joy.

JOKE   *JOHK*   *noun*

Originally spelled *joque* in English, this word comes from the Latin *iocus*. The Latin *iocus* means "joke," but it was also a word for a game or a playful activity. It originally comes from a Proto-Indo-European root meaning "to speak."

Example: Q: Where does a queen keep her armies? A: In her sleevies!

JUDGMENT   *JUJ-ment*   *noun*

A judgment is a decision you make about someone or something. It originally comes from the Latin *iudicare*, meaning "to examine officially." The Latin *iudicem*, or the person making the judgment, is a combination of the Latin *ius*, meaning "law," and *dicere*, meaning "to say." This is because a judge is someone who speaks or makes decisions based on the law. It's important to remember that not all judgments are fair or true.

JUSTICE   *JUSS-tiss*   *noun*

Our modern idea of justice, with courts, judges, juries, and lawyers, is based on ideas written by Greek philosophers. "Justice" was adopted directly from Old French, which evolved from the Latin *iustitia*, meaning "righteousness" or "fairness."

Example: The baker received justice when the judge sentenced the bread thief to two weeks of community service.

KARATE

Read more on page 124

K

KALEIDOSCOPE   *kuh-LIY-duh-skohp*   noun

Have you ever looked through a kaleidoscope? It's a tube-shaped device that uses mirrors and colorful decorative items to create visual illusions. The kaleidoscope was invented by a Scottish scientist named David Brewster who studied optics, or the way we see things. The word literally means "observer of beautiful things" or "an instrument for seeing beautiful shapes," from the Greek *kalos* ("beautiful"), *eidos* ("shape"), and *-scope* ("a tool for seeing").

KARAOKE   *KAIR-ee-oh-kee*   noun

If you've ever been to a karaoke party, you know that you sing the lyrics of your favorite songs while the melody plays in the background. Karaoke is a combination of the Japanese words *kara*, meaning "empty," and *oke*, meaning "orchestra."

KARATE

ker-AH-tee

noun

Karate is a Japanese fighting style that involves no weapons, just your hands and feet. In Japanese, it means "empty hand" or "bare hand."

KAYAK   *KIY-ak*   noun

A kayak is a small boat similar to a canoe. They were originally used by Inuit people, who made them by stretching sealskins over wooden frames. The Eskimo word *qayaq* literally means "small boat of skins."

KENNEL   *KEN-ull*   *noun*

When you go on vacation, you might take your dog to a kennel, where your dog will be kept safe until you return. Kennel comes from its French variation, *chenil*, which is originally from the Latin word for dog, *canis*.

KERFUFFLE   *kur-FUFF-uhl*   *noun*

"Ker-" is a funny prefix in the English language, often used to make a word more exaggerated. You see it in words like "kersplat" or "kerfuffle," which is based on the Scottish verb *fuffle*, meaning "to throw into disorder." It was originally spelled *curfufle* and was used to describe a very fluffy lacy collar around a gentleman's neck.

Example: It caused a kerfuffle when the dog broke out of its kennel!

KHAKI   *KAK-ee*   *adjective*

Your school uniform might require you to wear khaki pants or a khaki skirt. This word is originally from the Urdu language, which is spoken in Pakistan and India. It means "dusty" because of its color. Khaki was first used for the uniforms of British soldiers in India because it camouflages well with dusty landscapes.

KILOMETER   *kill-AW-meet-ur*   *noun*

A kilometer is a unit of measurement that equals 1,000 meters. "Kilo" comes from the Greek *khilioi*, meaning "thousand." "Meter" comes from the Greek *metron*, meaning "measure." So, a kilometer is 1,000 of this unit of measurement.

KITE   KIYT   _noun_

A kite is a small type of hawk. It's also the name of a toy you fly in the park. Both originally come from the Old English _cyta_, which is meant to imitate the sound the bird makes. The name of the toy also comes from the name of the bird because it hovers in the air just like one of these birds.

KLEPTOMANIA   KLEP-toh-may-nee-uh   _noun_

Someone who has kleptomania sometimes has an irresistible urge to steal things. It is formed by the Greek _kleptein_, meaning "to steal" or "to act secretly," and the Latin _mania_, meaning "madness" or "enthusiasm."

KNACK   NAK   _noun_

If you have a knack for something, you're naturally good at it. It was originally a word for a trick used to deceive others. It is thought to be related to older German and Middle English words for "to crack," perhaps like snapping your fingers, or in the sense of crack as "top-notch," like the phrase "crack team," meaning a skilled team.

Example: She had a knack for science, but she also studied hard to create cool experiments.

KNIGHT   NITE   _noun_

In Old English, a knight, or _cniht_, wasn't the noble warrior we think of today. Instead, he was a young boy who was an attendant or helper to someone noble. In the 1300s, when the code of conduct called "chivalry" was common practice, a knight came to be specifically a word for someone who serves a king. Knights soon began to play an important role in major battles, and over time, knights became associated with bravery and lordly manners.

KNIT   *NIT*   *verb*

If you've ever seen someone knitting, you know that they use two needles to make a series of interconnected loops. With time and practice, this can make a whole sweater or blanket! The word most likely comes from the Old English *cnotta*, meaning "a knot."

KNOW   *NOH*   *verb*

The earliest form of this ancient word was *cnawan* in Old English, which meant "to notice that two things are the same." Another word, *tocnawan*, was the ability to tell two things apart. This evolved into the ability to understand that something was true, and then to understand how to do something.

KNUCKLE   *NUK-uhl*   *noun*

This word for the joints in your fingers comes from a Germanic root meaning "little bone."

KRAKEN   *KRAK-en*   *noun*

Release the kraken! This giant sea monster comes from Nordic sea myths, probably inspired by the rare moments when sailors spotted a giant squid. In a Norwegian dialect, the word *krake* means "crooked tree" or "stunted animal."

KUDOS   *KOO-doze*   *noun*

When you go above and beyond on a school project or score a goal at a sports event, your teacher or coach might say "kudos!" To "give you kudos" is a way of telling you "great job!" This word was adopted from the Greek *kydos*, meaning "glory" or "fame," and was often used in relation to warriors in battle.

Read more on page 132

L

LABORATORY   *LAB-ruh-tor-ee*   noun

A laboratory is a place where a scientist does their work. The word literally means "a place to do work," from the Medieval Latin *laboratorium*, meaning "a place to do labor." The base word is *labor*, meaning "work" or "toil," and the ending *-atorium* means a place where something is done.

LACKADAISICAL   *LAK-uh-dayz-ik-uhl*   adjective

To be lackadaisical is to be unenthusiastic or lazy about something. It can also mean to be overly sentimental about something, thinking fondly of the past. When people felt this way in the olden days, they would cry "Alack the day!" Others thought this was dramatic, so they combined the cry into one word to poke fun.

LACKLUSTER   *LAK-luss-tur*   adjective

To lack something is to have none of it. "Luster" means "shine," from the Latin *lustrare*, meaning "to brighten" or "to spread light over." So, something that is lackluster literally means "to lack shine," or to be dull or uninteresting.

LACROSSE   *luh-KROSS*   noun

The name of the sport lacrosse was borrowed from Canadian French. The full name was *jeu de la crosse*, or "game of the hooked sticks." However, the game was invented by Native Americans, who would play for two or three days in a row as part of a ceremony giving thanks to a creator god.

LANGUAGE   *LANG-widj*   *noun*

This word originally meant "conversation," or things that are said. It's from the Old French *langage*, which meant both "speech or words" and "a tribe or nation of people." The French comes from the Latin *lingua*, meaning "tongue" or "speech."

LASSO   *LASS-oh*   *noun*

Cowboys use this long rope with a loop to catch runaway cattle. It was adopted from the Spanish *lazo*, meaning "a snare" or "a slipknot," and originally comes from the same Latin source as "lace."

LAUGH   *LAFF*   *noun*

The Old English source of the word "laugh" looks a lot like the sound of someone laughing: It was spelled *hlihhan*, and it was probably an attempt to spell out the sound of laughter in writing before we landed on "hahaha."

LAVENDER   *LAV-ehn-dur*   *adjective/noun*

This word, which can refer to either the plant or the light purple color, most likely comes from the Latin *lavare*, meaning "to wash." This is because lavender flowers were used as a perfume for bathing and for washing fabric.

LEGEND   *LEDJ-und*   *noun*

This word comes from the Medieval Latin *legenda*, which referred to stories read aloud in churches. It literally meant "things that were read." The older Latin *legendus* could also mean "to gather or collect," which gives our modern word the sense of someone gathering stories to put in a collection.

LEGISLATION   *LEDJ-iss-lay-shun*   *noun*

When lawmakers (like congresspeople and senators) pass new laws,
it's called "legislation." This word comes from the Latin *legislationem*,
literally meaning "to bring law." It more broadly refers to the process of
enacting a law.

LEOTARD   *LEE-oh-tard*   *noun*

A leotard is a tight piece of clothing worn by gymnasts and other athletes. The word comes from the name of Jules Léotard, an acrobat
who was the first trapeze artist and is credited with inventing that style
of performance.

LEPRECHAUN   *LEP-ri-kawn*   *noun*

A leprechaun is a small Irish fairy or sprite that tends to play mischievous tricks. Its name comes from the Old Irish *luchorpan*, a combination
of *lu*, meaning "small," and *corp*, meaning "body."

LETHAL   *LEE-thull*   *adjective*

If something is lethal, you'd better watch out—because it can kill you!
The word comes from *lethum* or *letum*, a Latin word for "death" that
was related to the Lethe, a mythical river in the Greek underworld.

LETHARGY   *LEH-thur-jee*   *noun*

Feeling unwilling to move or do anything is lethargy. The word is a combination of the Greek *lethe*, meaning "forgetfulness," and *argos*, meaning
"idle." It first described someone who became so forgetful that they
no longer moved or did much. It was also associated with the Lethe, a
mythical river in Hades (the underworld) that caused forgetfulness in
anyone who drank from it.

LEVITATE
lev-ih-TAYT verb

To make something levitate is to cause it to float in the air. You'll often hear about levitating in stories about magic. It comes from the Latin word *levitas*, meaning "lightness," as in something that weighs very little. This word is also related to the English word "levity," meaning a light and pleasant feeling as if you're so happy that you're floating on air.

Example: The magician made the bunny levitate over the hat!

LIBERTY
LIB-ur-tee

noun

Have you ever seen the Statue of Liberty? It is a symbol of freedom for people who come from countries that may have strict or oppressive governments. Liberty is having the freedom to do what you wish and not be controlled by anyone else. The English word and its Old French predecessor, *liberte*, both come from the Latin *liber*, meaning "free."

LIEUTENANT
LOO-ten-ant noun

The role of a lieutenant is to serve as a military officer, usually directly under a commander or a captain. The title was adopted from French and literally means "placeholder," from *lieu*, meaning "place," and *tenir*, meaning "to hold."

LIQUID
LIK-wid adjective/noun

A liquid is a substance that is neither a solid nor a gas, but something in between. Liquids are capable of being poured and can run like a river. It comes from the Latin *liqui*, meaning "to melt or flow."

LITERACY   *LIT-err-uh-see*   *noun*

Literacy is a very important skill that will help you throughout your life. The good news is, if you're reading this, you already have it! Someone who is literate can read and write, while someone who is illiterate cannot. This word comes from the Latin *literatus*, meaning "educated" or "knowing letters," from the base word *littera*, or "letter."

LITERATURE   *LIT-ur-uh-chur*   *noun*

Today, we think of literature as a word for classic books like *Treasure Island, Winnie-the-Pooh,* or *The Wind in the Willows.* In the 15th century, this English word meant "book learning," or learning from books rather than learning a trade like blacksmithing or shoe-making. It comes from the Latin *literatura*, meaning "learning" or "grammar." It is originally from the Latin *littera*, meaning "a letter of the alphabet."

LOBSTER   *LOB-stur*   *noun*

These animals get their name from the Latin *locusta*, meaning "locust" or "grasshopper," because they look similar to these land-dwelling insects. Its spelling is also probably influenced by the Old English *lobbe*, meaning "spider."

LOGIC   *LODJ-ik*   *noun*

Logic is the way you use your reasoning to think about something or come to a decision about it. In Ancient Greece, when people debated for fun, logic was known as the "art of reason" (*logike techne*), or the practice of telling the difference between what is true or real and what is false or imaginary. It originally comes from the Greek *logos*, meaning "reason."

Example: My sister tried to explain her math trick for multiplying large numbers, but I couldn't understand her logic.

LULLABY *LULL-uh-by* *noun*

A lullaby, or a song people sing to babies to help them sleep, comes from *lollai* or *lullay*, which were both common words in Middle English nursery songs.

LUNATIC *LOON-uh-tik* *noun*

This word is often used as an insult today, describing someone who thinks or acts strangely. You might be surprised to learn that "lunatic" and "lunacy" were once medical terms that doctors and philosophers used for people who struggled with their mental health. These doctors used the term for people who they believed were being influenced by changes in the moon. "Lunar" means anything related to the moon. "Lunatic" comes from the Latin *lunaticus*, which literally means "moonstruck." Today we know that mental problems aren't caused by nature in this way.

LUXURY *LUG-zhur-ee* *adjective/noun*

Luxury is the state of having far more than what you need to survive. This might include excessive comfort, food, or activities. The word comes from the Latin *luxus*, meaning "dislocated," just like a joint when you bend it too far. This sense of "too far" or "too much" led to its use as a word for an excessive lifestyle full of pleasurable things.

MERMAID

Read more on page 141

M

MAFIA *MAH-fee-ah* *noun*
Many popular movies have been made about the American Prohibition era that involved the Mafia. Prohibition made it illegal to sell alcoholic drinks, but the Mafia was made up of Italian gangsters who sold the drinks anyway. The name is Sicilian and means "boldness," but it probably originally comes from the Arabic *mahjas*, "aggressively boasting."

MAGIC *MADJ-ik* *noun*
In ancient times, it was thought that priests and religious leaders had the power to talk with the gods, sometimes even making supernatural things happen. That's why "magic" originally comes from the Greek *magos*, a word for priests and educated people who supposedly had such powers. Over time, the concept of magic evolved to include anyone who was thought to be able to control spiritual and supernatural forces and creatures.

MAGNET *MAG-nut* *noun*
A magnet is a substance that attracts iron and steel, and its name comes from the region where it was discovered: Magnesia. This part of Greece was a known place where one could find lodestones, or pieces of the mineral we now called magnetite that attracts other metals.

MAGNIFICENT *mag-NIH-fuh-sent* *adjective*
Imagine a legendary hero setting out on a great quest to conquer monsters, fight great battles, and save people who need help. That's the idea behind "magnificent." It comes from the Latin *magnificus*, literally meaning "doing great deeds," from the Latin *magnus*, meaning "great," and *facere*, meaning "to make" or "to do."

MAGNIFY   *MAG-nih-fiy*   verb

You might use a magnifying glass or telescope to expand an image of something too small to see clearly. In the 1300s this word was most often a religious term, so that to magnify was to tell stories glorifying a god or a person. It comes from the Latin *magnus*, meaning "great."

MALICE   *MAA-liss*   noun

You should watch out for anyone who is malicious, or full of malice, because they might have bad intentions or want to hurt you. This word comes from the Latin *malus*, meaning "bad" or "unpleasant." It shares an origin with the disease called malaria, which means "bad air."

MAMMOTH   *MAAM-uth*   noun/adjective

If you have heard of a "woolly mammoth," you may be able to visualize a huge animal with long tusks, maybe in the snow. A mammoth was a type of huge, shaggy elephant that looked just like that and went extinct about 4,000 years ago. Their remains have been found perfectly preserved in the icy regions of Siberia. The name, which can also be used as an adjective meaning "huge" or "massive," comes from a Russian word from this region, probably meaning "earth" because their remains were dug up from the earth. Some early discoverers even thought that they lived underground and dug tunnels like giant moles.

MANIPULATE   *muh-NIP-yoo-late*   verb

To manipulate something is to change its shape or to mold it with your hands, like clay. It's also a word that means changing a situation to benefit yourself. Etymologically, this word is all about hands and handling things. It comes from the Latin *manipulus*, meaning "a handful," and is made up of *manus*, meaning "hand," and *plere*, meaning "to fill."

Example: I tried to manipulate my mom into letting me stay up later, but she was too clever for my tactics.

MANNEQUIN   *MAN-uh-kin*   *noun*

This name for a dummy that is used to display clothes was adopted from French in the early 1900s, but it originally comes from the Dutch *manneken*, which literally meant "little man."

MANTIS   *MAN-tiss*   *noun*

You've probably heard the term "praying mantis" before. This insect got its name because it looks wise, holding its front legs in a religious prayer-like position. The Greek word *mantis* means "seer" or "prophet." It comes from the word *mainesthai*, which means "to be inspired." In this context, "inspire" means "to fill the mind or heart," because it was thought that the Ancient Greek gods breathed visions and messages into the minds of prophets and seers.

MANUFACTURE   *MAN-yoo-FAK-churr*   *verb*

Have you ever seen a video of products or goods being made by machines in a factory? To manufacture an item is to make it, just like those machines do. But etymologically, manufacturing has nothing to do with making things using machines. The Latin *manufactura* was a word for making something by hand. It is made up of the Latin *manu*, meaning "hand," and *facere*, meaning "to make."

MARATHON   *MAIR-uh-thawn*   *noun*

This type of footrace is 26.2 miles long. In 490 BCE, there was a great battle between Persian and Athenian armies on a field called Marathon. When the Athenian army won the battle, an unknown runner ran roughly 25 miles back to Athens to report the news. The race was named after the runner when the Olympic Games, originally an ancient Greek tradition, were revived in 1896.

MARVELOUS   *MAR-vuh-liss*   adjective

A marvel, or something that is marvelous, looks so amazing that it's sure to bring a smile to your face. It comes from the Latin *mirus*, meaning "wonderful," and the Latin source originally comes from a Proto-Indo-European root meaning "to smile."

MASCOT   *MASS-kot*   noun

Mascots have been around for centuries, but they weren't always costumed characters that danced at sporting events. In the 1800s, it was a word (from the French word *mascotte*) for a good-luck charm or a person or fairy who brought good luck. Later, animals were associated with different sports teams as good-luck charms themselves, or as symbols that inspired the athletes to play with (for example) the fierceness of a tiger.

MASON   *MAYS-uhn*   noun

A mason is someone who cuts stone, makes bricks, and builds structures out of them. We get it from the Old French *maçon*, also meaning "stonemason," which originally came from a Proto-Indo-European root meaning "to knead" or "to fit."

MATHEMATICS   *MATH-uh-ma-tiks*   noun

The first people to use math beyond basic counting were the Babylonians and Egyptians around 3000 BCE. This area of study was once broader than it is now, encompassing science, math, astronomy, and sometimes other forms of learning. Its Greek source *mathema* literally means "that which is learned."

MEDIOCRE   *MEE-dee-oh-kur*   adjective

Something mediocre isn't bad, but it isn't great either. It's just okay. It comes from the Latin *mediocris*, which was used the same way as the English word but literally meant "halfway up a mountain," from *medius*, or "middle," and *ocris*, or "jagged mountain."

MELANCHOLY   *MEL-un-call-ee*   *adjective*

Someone who is melancholy may be in a sad and gloomy mood. Before modern medicine, it was thought that the amounts of different fluids in our bodies could change our moods. For example, if you had too much blood, doctors thought you were more prone to anger. Sadness was thought to come from a substance known as black bile, or *melankholia* in Greek. The Greek word is made up of the elements *melas*, meaning "black," and *khole*, meaning "bile." Today we know that black bile isn't a real substance and that the things that change your mood are much more complex.

MENTAL   *MEN-tuhl*   *adjective*

This word refers to anything having to do with your thoughts, mind, or intellect. It comes from the Late Latin *mentalis*, meaning "of the mind." It is originally from the Latin *mens*, or "mind."

MENTOR   *MEN-tohr*   *noun*

A mentor is a trusted, experienced person who helps you when you need guidance or advice. In *The Odyssey*, a famous epic poem about the journey of a hero named Odysseus, the main character's best friend was also an adviser to his son. This man's name was Mentor. This story is one of the most famous stories in all of written history and inspired the common use of the word today. It is thought to originally come from a root meaning "one who thinks."

MERCENARY   *MER-sun-air-ee*   *noun*

A mercenary is a soldier who will fight in exchange for money, rather than because of any loyalty to the people or country they are fighting for. It comes from the Latin *merces*, meaning "pay" or "reward."

MERMAID

MUR-mayd

noun

This word for a mythical half-fish, half-woman literally means "girl of the sea," with the first part from the Middle English *mere*, meaning "sea or lake."

METAPHOR   *MET-uh-for*   *noun*

A metaphor is a direct comparison that often uses the word "is." For example, you might have heard or read the phrases "The snow is a white blanket on the ground" or "Life is a roller coaster." The snow isn't truly a white blanket, but it looks like one. Life isn't really a roller coaster, but it can feel like one with its ups and downs. The word comes from the Greek *metaphora*, meaning "a transfer," or literally "a carrying across," from *meta-*, "over, across," and *pherein*, "to carry." The comparison "carries" the definition across so that you understand the intended meaning of the words rather than the literal meaning.

METEOR   *MEET-ee-or*   *noun*

This word for a shooting star comes from the Greek word *meteoron*, which literally means "a thing high up." In the 15th century, "meteor" could refer to anything that appeared naturally in the sky. This includes tornados, rainbows, snow, and lightning, as well as asteroids and shooting stars. That's why the weather reporter on the news is called a meteorologist, and why "meteorology" refers to the study of the weather and atmospheric conditions.

METROPOLIS *MET-raw-poh-liss* noun

Today we think of a metropolis as a big, bustling city. In Greek, it means "mother city," from *meter*, or "mother," and *polis*, or "city." During the height of the Roman Empire, they would claim or colonize an area of a country, establish a capital city, and control the smaller colonies around it from that city—the metropolis. In English, it was also used as a religious term for a city where a high-ranking bishop would live and control the bishops in the provinces around the city.

MINIATURE *MIN-ee-uh-chur* adjective

A miniature is a tiny version of something larger. You might expect the word to be closely related to words like "miniscule" (something very small) and "minor" (something smaller) that come from the Latin *minor*, meaning "small." But "miniature" comes from a slightly different source. The first things to be called "miniatures" were small drawings that were added to early, handwritten books and documents. They were small, but more importantly, they were named after their color. "Miniature" comes from the Latin *miniare*, meaning "to paint red," because these drawings were often made in ink from a red material called *minium*.

MIRACLE *MEER-uh-kuhl* noun

This word for a pleasant and extraordinary event comes from the Latin *mirus*, meaning "wonderful," astonishing," or "amazing." The Latin source originally comes from a Proto-Indo-European root meaning "to smile."

MISCHIEF *MISS-chiff* noun

This word for causing trouble used to be a much stronger word meaning "evil," "wickedness," or "misfortune." It comes from the Old French *meschever,* meaning "to bring grief," or literally "happening badly." The second part, *chever*, originally comes from the Latin *caput*, or "head," because of the sense that something that happens to you "comes to a head," or reaches a point of crisis.

MISERY MIZ-ur-ee *noun*

To be miserable is to feel great sadness and distress. It comes from the Latin *miseria*, meaning "wretchedness" or deep unhappiness. This is also the source of the word "miser," which we use as a word for someone who jealously guards their money, but it originally meant someone very unhappy.

MNEMONIC nuh-MAWN-ik *adjective*

A mnemonic device is one that helps you remember something. For example, "My Very Educated Mother Just Served Us Nine Pizzas" might help you remember the names of the planets in our solar system, as well as their order from the sun: Mercury, Venus, Earth, Mars, Jupiter, Saturn, Uranus, Neptune, and (the dwarf planet) Pluto. The word "mnemonic" originally comes from the Greek *mnasthai*, meaning "to remember."

MODERN MAW-durn *adjective*

This word describes things that have happened in recent history or are happening right now. The word originally comes from the Latin *modo*, meaning "just now."

Example: Modern technology has changed the way people communicate.

MOLAR MOW-lur *noun*

A molar is any of your large back teeth used for crushing and grinding food. It was named after the Latin *mola*, or "millstone," a large rolling stone used to grind grain into flour.

MONASTERY MAWN-uh-stair-ee *noun*

A monastery is a place where monks and other religious people go to live in quiet peace and think about their beliefs or existence. It comes from the Greek *monasterion*, meaning "to live alone," which is made up of *monos*, or "alone," and the ending *-terion*, which meant a place to do something. So, a monastery is literally a place for being alone.

MONEY   *MUN-ee*   *noun*

In Latin, *Moneta* was a title or name from the Roman goddess Juno. There was a temple dedicated to her on the Capitoline Hill, and nearby was the place where coins were made and stamped. After that, many places for coining money were named after Moneta. It's this tradition that ultimately gave us the word "money."

MONOPOLY   *muh-NAW-poh-lee*   *noun*

This word isn't just the name of a popular board game. It's also a word for a company or group that owns all of the businesses that sell one type of product. For example, if a company has a monopoly on books, it means that company owns all of the stores that sell books. This word comes from the Greek *monos*, meaning "single" or "only," and *polein*, meaning "to sell."

Example: My neighbor, the only one with the huge lemon tree, had a monopoly on fresh lemonade stands in our town.

MONOTONY   *muh-NAW-toh-nee*   *noun*

Monotony is when the same boring thing happens over and over again without a break. It comes from the Greek *monotonos*, meaning "of the same tone," as in a sound that repeats without change. It's made up of the elements *monos*, meaning "single" or "only," and *tonos*, meaning "tone" or "sound."

Example: In class today, we had to do 50 exercises that were all very similar. I thought I would fall asleep because of the monotony.

MONSTER   *MON-stur*   *noun*

Today we think of monsters as being dangerous, scary creatures or movie villains. To the Romans, *monstrum* meant an omen from the gods, especially one foretelling something bad. The modern sense of the word came from the fact that unusually large or deformed animals were almost always considered bad omens.

MOSQUITO   *MUSS-kee-toh*   *noun*

The name of these bloodsucking insects was borrowed directly from Spanish. Mosquito means "little gnat" or "little fly," from the Latin *musca*, meaning "fly," and the Spanish ending *-ito*, which is a diminutive, meaning that it makes the base word smaller.

MOTIVATE   *MOH-ti-vait*   *verb*

If you feel motivated, it means that you're ready to get things done, go places, and overcome challenges. Based on the Latin origin *motus*, meaning "motion," it indicates that you're literally ready to move forward.

MOXIE   *MOK-see*   *noun*

To have moxie is to be determined, to have the nerve to do something brave or independent. But "Moxie" was originally the brand name of a bitter-tasting soda called Moxie Nerve Food! First sold as medicine in the 1800s, it was said to help you "build up your nerve," or make you brave. The brand name may be from an Abenaki word meaning "dark water," used in Maine lake and river names.

MULTILINGUAL   *MULL-tee-ling-wull*   *adjective*

Do you speak more than two languages? If so, that makes you multilingual! The first part of this word, *multi-*, means "many" and comes from the Latin word for "many," *multus*. The "lingual" part of the word comes from the Latin *lingua,* meaning "language," or literally "tongue" (because you use your tongue to speak). This word is also the source of "linguistics," or the study of languages.

Example: My friend speaks English, Arabic, and French. He is multilingual!

MUSCLE   *MUSS-uhl*   *noun*

"Muscle" comes from the Latin word for muscle, *musculus*, which is also translated as "little mouse." It comes from the Latin base word *mus*, meaning "mouse." Muscles are named after mice because it was thought that flexing your muscles made it look like mice were crawling under your skin!

MUSEUM   *MYOO-zee-uhm*   *noun*

This word for a building containing a collection of historic or artistic exhibits comes from the Greek *mouseion*, meaning "place of study" or "library." Before that, though, it was a Greek word for a temple to the Muses. The Muses were goddesses in Greek mythology who were thought to inspire people to create art, music, literature, and scientific inventions.

MUTATION   *MYOO-tay-shun*   *noun*

In evolution, a mutation is when one animal has a difference from others in its species. Sometimes this difference allows a species to evolve. According to research by the naturalist Charles Darwin, a bird with a mutation that makes its beak better at cracking open seeds is more likely to survive and have babies, so future generations of birds might end up with these same seed-cracking beaks. This word originally comes from the Latin *mutare*, meaning "to change."

MUTUAL   *MYOO-choo-uhl*   *adjective*

If you and your friend both respect one another, your respect is mutual, meaning that you both give and receive it. This word comes from the Latin *mutuus*, meaning "something done in exchange" or something done in return.

MYSTERY *MISS-tuh-ree* noun

A mystery is something that is unknown or a question that is unsolved. It originally comes from the French *mistere*, meaning "secret" or "hidden meaning." The earlier Latin *mysterium* and the Greek *mysterion* were words for secret rituals and sacrifices by religious groups that only accepted initiated members.

MYTH *MITH* noun

The myth, or *mythos*, was an important part of Greek history and culture. Before books were common, when many people could not read or write, storytellers would travel from town to town sharing stories of great historic moments and fictional tales. The history they shared was intertwined with sagas of gods, goddesses, heroes, and fantastic creatures.

NOVEL

Read more on page 154

N

NARCISSISM   *NAR-suh-siz-uhm*   noun

Narcicissm is when someone is self-centered and likes themself more than anyone else. This word comes from the Greek story of Narcissus, a beautiful young man who looked at his own reflection in the water and fell in love with what he saw. Unable to look away from his reflection, he was transformed into a white and gold flower. There is a type of flower called narcissus named after him today.

NARRATOR   *NAIR-ate-or*   noun

The narrator of a story is the person telling it, often a fictional character whose perspective you see the story through. In Latin, the same word also meant "historian." It originally comes from the Latin *narrare*, meaning "to tell or relate (a story)."

NASTY   *NASS-tee*   adjective

Some etymologists believe that this word is a shortening of the Old French word *villenastre*, meaning "villainous, infamous, or bad." To be "nasty" literally means to behave like a villain, but it's more common to use this word as a substitute for "bad." Food can taste nasty, or you can have a nasty cold. Many women after the 2016 presidential election also "co-opted" the word, meaning that to take the negative power out of the word, they started to embrace it in a positive way ("Nasty Woman").

NATURAL   *NATCH-ur-ul*   adjective/noun

Your natural qualities are the ones you were born with, such as your hair color or texture, as well as things that you seem to be inherently good at. The natural world is anything that occurs without the influence of humankind. This word, which is related to "nature," comes from the Latin *naturalis*, meaning "by birth."

NAUSEA   *NAW-zee-uh*   *noun*

If you're nauseated, your stomach is upset, and you may feel like you're going to vomit. Many people feel seasick when they're on a boat thanks to the rocking motion of the waves. That's why "nausea" means "ship-sickness," from the Greek *naus*, or "ship."

NAVIGATE   *NAV-uh-gait*   *verb*

To navigate is to find your way somewhere using a map or directions. In the 1500s, to "navigate" meant "to sail somewhere in a ship." A navigator was someone who made sure the ship was going the right way on the open seas by following maps of the stars and landmarks. This word originally comes from the Latin *navigare*, meaning "to sail" or "to steer a ship." It is made up of the elements *navis*, meaning "ship" and *agere*, meaning "to set in motion" or "to drive forward."

NEFARIOUS   *nuh-FAIR-ee-uss*   *adjective*

A nefarious villain is one who is evil and wicked. This word comes from the Latin *nefas*, meaning "crime," which is formed by *ne-*, or "not," and *fas*, or "lawful, right."

NEGLECT   *nuh-GLEKT*   *noun/verb*

To neglect something is to pay no attention to it. It comes from the Latin *neglectus*, which literally meant "not to pick up." It is made from the Latin *nec*, meaning "not," and *legere*, meaning "to pick up."

NEIGHBOR   *NAY-bur*   *noun*

Your neighbors are the people who are physically beside you or who live close to you. This word literally means "near-dweller," an adaptation of the Old English *neahgebur*, a combination of *neah*, meaning "near" and *gebur*, meaning "dweller."

NERD   *NURD*   *noun*

This word, spelled "nert" around 1940, was a slang version of the word "nut" (meaning a crazy person). By 1951 it had become college slang for a person who was very enthusiastic about a particular topic. It also appeared in the book *If I Ran the Zoo* by Dr. Seuss (1950) as a name for an imaginary creature.

NEUROLOGIST   *NOOR-aw-loh-jist*   *noun*

The human body can feel things thanks to the nervous system, the network of nerves and cells that allows you to feel things. A doctor who studies the nervous system, or neurology, is called a neurologist. This name of the person and the topic they study comes from the Greek *neuro-*, meaning "nerves" or "the nervous system," and *-logia*, meaning "study of."

NICHE   *NITCH, NEESH*   *noun*

A niche is a small nook in a wall. It can also mean a particular area or skill that someone is knowledgeable about. For example, a doctor who sees many patients with a rare disease has a niche because she knows more about it than other doctors and is seen as an expert. One theory says that "niche" comes from the Old French *nichier*, meaning "to build a nest, originally from the Latin *nidus*, meaning "nest."

NICKELODEON   *NIK-uh-loh-dee-uhn*   *noun*

Before this was the name of a TV network, it was a word for a movie or motion-picture theater or a jukebox. "Nickelodeon" is made from "nickel" (like the coin) and the Greek word *oideion*, a type of roofed-over theater where music was performed. The idea was that visitors could pay a nickel to see a movie or play a song.

NIGHTMARE   *NITE-mayr*   noun

Nightmares are scary dreams that happen at night while we're asleep. The "mare" part comes from *mera* or *mære*—Old English names for a type of goblin or demon that was thought to cause bad dreams.

NINCOMPOOP   *NIN-kum-poop*   noun

A nincompoop is someone who isn't very intelligent. Its origin isn't certain, but it might come from the Latin phrase *non compos mentis*, or "not having the power of the mind," a term used in court for someone who was mentally unfit or insane.

NOBLE   *NOH-bull*   adjective/noun

A nobleperson was one of the members of a royal family that ruled over a community of lower-ranking people. It comes from the Latin *nobilis*, meaning "well-known" or "famous." Used as an adjective, it means "having outstanding, brave, or honorable qualities."

NOCTURNAL   *nok-TUR-nuhl*   adjective

Nocturnal animals, like bats and owls, are those that come out only at night. It originally comes from the Latin *nocturnus*, which means "belonging to the night." It is made up of *nox*, or "night," and *-urnus*, a suffix that creates adjectives related to time. The opposite of "nocturnal" is "diurnal." This refers to animals that come out in the daytime. Here, *nox* is replaced by the Latin *dies*, or "day."

NOMINATE   *NOM-in-ate*   verb

When you nominate someone to do something, like run for president or lead the school student council, you're naming them as the one you want to be chosen for the role. This word comes from the Latin *nominare*, meaning "to name" or "to call by name."

NONCHALANT   *NAWN-shuh-lawnt*   *adjective*

Someone who is nonchalant behaves in a casual, unconcerned way. This word was adopted directly from French and is a combination of *non-*, or "not," and *chaloir*, meaning "to have concern for." The second part is originally from the Latin *calere*, meaning "to be hot," because passion and care are associated with heat. So, the word itself implies "to have no heat or passion for (something or someone)."

Example: After studying for many hours, he was nonchalant about the pop quiz.

NORMAL   *NOR-muhl*   *adjective*

This common word comes from the Latin *normalis*, which literally meant "made according to a carpenter's square." A carpenter's square is a tool used to measure exact corners for building projects. It helps them ensure that woodworking projects end up the same size and built with the same angles. Today's meaning comes from the idea of anything that fits into common patterns and expectations.

NOSTALGIA   *nuh-STAHL-djah*   *noun*

Nostalgia is remembering a happy moment, a person, or a place from your past. You might even feel a little bit sad that you can't experience it again. It was originally translated into Modern Latin from the German *heimweh*, or "homesickness." The translation was formed of the Greek *nostos*, meaning "homecoming," and *algos*, meaning "pain or grief."

NOVEL

NAH-vull

adjective/noun

A novel is a book-length fictional (made-up) story. The first official novel was *Don Quixote* by Miguel de Cervantes, published in 1605. At that time, novels were called "romances," even if the story wasn't about love. The name "novel" comes from the Latin *novella*, or a "new thing." (In English, "novella" is a term for a short novel.) When used as an adjective, "novel" describes something new.

Example (adjective): He had a novel idea to put yogurt on toast. It was delicious!

NUANCE   NOO-ahnss   noun

Nuance is a slight difference between two things. It was first used to describe a color that was slightly different from another, such as royal blue compared to navy blue. It originally comes from the Latin *nubes*, meaning a cloud or mist that might shade or cover a landscape, slightly changing its color.

NUCLEAR   NOO-clee-arr   adjective

This word usually refers to a type of energy that is created when atoms split apart or combine. Atoms are the smallest microscopic pieces of any element (like hydrogen, oxygen, gold, or silver). The center of an atom is called the "nucleus." This originally comes from the Latin *nucula*, or "little nut." *Nucle* was also a Middle English word for a kernel or seed.

OTTER

Read more on page 161

O

OASIS   *oh-AY-siss*   *noun*

An oasis is a patch of water and trees in the middle of a desert land-scape. It most likely comes from an ancient word meaning "dwelling place," because an oasis would be much easier to live in than a harsh desert.

OBEY   *oh-BAY*   *verb*

Today, this word means to carry out the orders of a person in charge, or simply to do what you are told, but its meaning was originally a bit simpler. It comes from the Latin *oboedire*, meaning "to pay attention to."

OBNOXIOUS   *uhb-NAWK-shiss*   *adjective*

You might call a little brother or sister obnoxious when they're being very unpleasant. In Latin, it was a much more serious term. The word described someone who was put in harm's way or was hurt by someone else, from *ob-*, meaning "toward," and *noxa*, meaning "injury."

OBSERVE   *ob-ZERV*   *verb*

To observe means to watch something. It also means to participate in a tradition. Someone who is Catholic observes the tradition of fasting during Lent, or someone who is Muslim observes Ramadan. In both cases, this word suggests paying attention to something and noticing it. It comes from the Latin *observare*, meaning "to pay attention to," "to watch over," or "to guard." It is made up of the elements *ob*, meaning "in front of" or "in the direction of," and *servare*, meaning "to watch" or "to keep safe."

OBVIOUS   *AHB-vee-uss*   *adjective*

Something that is obvious is so easy to see or understand that it's more difficult to avoid it than to see it. You might even say it's right under your nose. The word comes from the Latin *obviam*, meaning "in the way" or right in front of you. The Latin is made up of the prefix *ob-*, meaning "in front of" or "against," and *viam*, meaning "way."

OCCULT   *uh-KULT*   *adjective*

This word is usually associated with witches, sorcerers, and other people who use and believe in magic and mysticism. It once had a simpler meaning: secret knowledge, from the Latin *occultus*, meaning "hidden" or "covered over."

OCCUPY   *AWK-yoo-piy*   *verb*

To occupy a space is to live or settle in it. It has often been used histori-cally as a word for an army's movement into a new territory as it claims the land and the people there. It comes from the Latin *occupare*, meaning "to take over" or "to seize."

OCEAN   *OH-shun*   *noun*

Some ancient cultures believed that the Earth was a flat disk, and all of the land was surrounded by a huge salt river or sea that was called *okeanos*. It was those mythical waters that inspired the word "ocean."

OCTOPUS   *AWK-toh-puss*   *noun*

These sea creatures, known for their intelligence, are named for their many arms. The Greek *oktopous* means "eight-foot." It is made up of the elements *okto*, or "eight," and *pous*, meaning "foot."

OFFEND   *UH-fend*   *verb*

Offending someone today usually means insulting things about them that they sometimes cannot change. It comes from the Latin *offendere*, meaning "to strike against."

Example: I didn't mean to offend my brother when I pointed out the hole in his favorite jacket, but he told me later that I did.

OGRE   *OH-gur*   *noun*

The fictional creatures called ogres get their name from Old English fairy tales. In these stories, including *The Tales of Mother Goose*, the word was spelled *hogre*. It is thought that the name was inspired by the Italian word *orco*, meaning "demon" or "monster." *Orco* comes from Orcus, a name for the Roman and Greek underworld.

OLYMPICS   *oh-LIM-piks*   *noun*

The Olympic Games are a world-celebrated sporting event that happens every two to four years. They are named after Olympia, a town in Greece where the first Olympic Games happened. The area is dedicated to the god Zeus and is located near Mount Olympus, a mountain that was thought to be the home of the gods.

OMNISCIENT   *ahm-NIH-shent*   *adjective*

Someone who is omniscient knows everything there is to know (all-knowing). It is formed by the Latin *omni-*, meaning "all," and *scientia*, meaning "knowledge." The prefix *omni-* can also be found in words like "omnipotent" (all-powerful) and "omnivorous" (referring to species that eat both plants and meat).

ONOMATOPOEIA   *AWN-uh-MAH-tuh-PEE-yuh*   noun
Onomatopoeia is when a word sounds like what it means, like pow, clang, thump, zap, or boom. It comes from the Greek *onomatopoiia*, meaning "to make the name (of a word)." The Greek is made up of the elements *onoma*, meaning "name," and *poiein*, meaning "to make."

OPAQUE   *OH-payk*   adjective
This word is the opposite of "transparent" or "clear." If something is opaque, you cannot see through it. It comes from the Latin *opacus*, meaning "shaded" or "dark."

Example: The glass window was opaque, so I couldn't see through it very well.

OPOSSUM   *uh-PAH-suhm*   noun
These animals look like large rats, although they are actually marsupials like kangaroos and koalas. Their name comes from an Algonquian word meaning "white animal" because their fur is often white or light gray.

OPPORTUNITY   *AW-pur-TOO-nih-tee*   noun
Once, the United States was called the Land of Opportunity because poor or suffering people could cross the oceans to find new work and new lives. Imagine being one of those people, giving up everything you knew, sailing for weeks on a ship, looking ahead. It comes from the Latin phrase *ob portum*, meaning "coming toward a port," just like these people would see a port ahead of them—a new life to aim for.

OPPRESS   oh-PRESS   *verb*

To oppress is to restrict someone from doing or saying something. A ruler who oppresses people treats them very badly, enforcing rules that make them feel overwhelmed or pushed down. This word originally comes from the Latin *opprimere*, meaning "to press against" or "to press down." The first part of the word comes from *ob*, which usually means "in the direction of," but suggests "against" in this case. The second part is from the Latin *premerre*, meaning "to press."

Example: The teacher oppressed the students by not letting them play outside.

OPTIMIST   AWP-tuh-mist   *noun*

An optimist always sees the positive in every situation, even when things are difficult. The word comes from the Modern Latin *optimum*, also a word in English, meaning "the greatest good" or "the best." The word became popular thanks to a philosopher named Gottfried Leibniz, who thought that our universe was the best possible one that could have been created.

ORANGUTAN   oh-RANG-oo-tan   *noun*

The name of these highly intelligent great apes originally comes from the Malay name for them, *orang utan*, meaning "man of the woods." Dutch explorers learned the word from people living on the island of Java in Indonesia and brought it back to Europe in the late 1600s.

ORBIT   OHR-bit   *noun/verb*

Today we think of an orbit as the path the planets take when circling the sun. The original Latin *orbita* was a word for the rut in the ground left by a wagon wheel, probably because "orb" was a word for anything circular like a wheel or a hoop. Later, "orb" (*orbem* in Latin) came to mean something that was spherical—not just a flat circle, but a round ball like a planet or an eye.

ORTHODONTIST   OR-tho-DON-tist   noun

An orthodontist is a special kind of dentist who focuses on straightening your teeth. (This is the doctor to give you braces!) The name literally means "someone who straightens teeth," from the Greek *ortho-*, meaning "straight," and *odontos,* meaning "tooth."

OSTRACIZE   AWS-truh-size   verb

To ostracize someone is to purposely leave someone out of a group, forcing them to be alone. It comes from the name of a practice in ancient Athens called *ostrakizein.* At that time, if someone was behaving badly, the townspeople would gather together. Anyone who thought the unpleasant person was acting against the good of the town would write the name of that person on a shard of a broken pot. If enough people wrote the person's name, the person would be banished for 10 years. The word, then, comes from *ostrakon*, meaning "tile" or "shard of a broken pot."

OTTER
AW-tur
noun
These playful animals get their name from the Greek *udros*, meaning "water creature." In seventeenth-century English, sea otters were also sometimes known as "sea-apes" because they were thought to resemble monkeys.

OXYMORON   AWK-see-mohr-awn   noun

An oxymoron is a phrase that combines two words that seem to go against each other. Some examples include "jumbo shrimp," "bittersweet," or "old news." The word "oxymoron" itself is an etymological oxymoron, a combination of the Greek *oxys*, meaning "sharp," and *moros*, meaning "stupid" or "dull." (Someone who is called sharp is usually clever, while someone who is dull is not considered clever.)

PTERODACTYL

Read more on page 176

P

PACIFIC   *puh-SIF-ik*   *adjective*

The Pacific Ocean was named by the explorer Ferdinand Magellan, who found that the waters were less stormy than those in the Atlantic Ocean. Its name means peaceful, from the Latin base word *pax*, or "peace."

PAJAMAS   *puh-JAW-muhz*   *noun*

Pajamas are worn around the world! In Western countries, they are typically worn at night, but the word and the loose-fitting style originates from Indian daytime fashion. It most likely comes from the Persian *paejamah*, meaning "leg clothing."

PALACE   *PAL-ess*   *noun*

A palace is a grand building where royalty might live. It comes from the name of Mons Palatinus, or the Palatine Hill in Rome, which was the location of the famous emperor Augustus Caesar's home—the first house to be called a palace.

PALINDROME   *PAL-in-drohm*   *noun*

A palindrome is a word or phrase that is spelled the same backward and forward, like mom, kayak, noon, or level. The word literally means "a running back" or "a running again." It's from the Greek *palin*, meaning "back, again," and *dromos*, "a running."

PANIC   *PAN-ik*   *noun*

This word for intense fear comes from the name of the Greek god Pan, the god who reigned over the wild woods and fields. He was thought to cause sounds that would send herds of cattle and people into a state of crazed terror. The full Greek phrase for this terror was *panikon deima*, meaning "panic fright" or a fright caused by Pan.

PANORAMA   *PAN-uh-RAM-uh*   *noun*

A panoramic photo is one that shows a very wide view of the subject of the photo. A panorama was originally a type of painting done on the inside of a cylinder, or a large tube, so that it had no beginning and no end, and the viewer could be surrounded by the painting. The word comes from the Greek *pan-*, meaning "all," and *horama*, meaning "sight or spectacle," so the full word means "a complete view."

PANTS   *PANTS*   *noun*

"Pants" might seem like casual slang, but it has a cheerful history. The word is short for "pantaloons," a type of clothing named after a popular Italian comedic character named Pantaloun. Pantaloun wore snug red tights over his skinny legs and was named after a Christian saint, San Pantaleone, whose name is of Greek origin and means "all-compassionate."

PARAGRAPH   *PAIR-uh-graf*   *noun*

In the days when books were written by hand, the writer would note a new chapter or a change in subject by drawing a small symbol called a pilcrow (¶). This symbol is still used today to note a new paragraph, though mostly by editors. The Greek *paragraphein* means "to write by the side" because the symbol was originally drawn in the margin beside the text.

PARTICULAR   *par-TIK-yoo-lur*   *adjective*

Particular means "specific" or "focused on small details." It comes from the Latin *particula*, meaning a little bit or part of something, or a single grain of something like wheat or rice. The word "particle" comes from the same source.

PARTNER   *PART-nur*   *noun*

A partner is someone who supports a business or relationship equally. It can even be a word for someone's spouse or romantic companion. It comes from the Latin *partitionem*, meaning "a sharing."

PASSION   *PASH-un*   *noun*

Today we think of passion as being a positive thing. You might have passion for a subject or activity you care deeply about. Someone could have deep love and passion for a romantic partner. But the Late Latin source word *passionem* means "suffering." It came to mean suffering out of intense love for people or a higher power.

ROOT SPOTLIGHT: *PATH*

Review the definitions of these terms that include the element *path*.

- **SYMPATHY:** to understand someone else's feelings, often sadness after something bad happens to another person

- **EMPATHY:** the ability to feel the emotions of other people

- **APATHY:** having no feeling or emotion about a situation

What do they have in common? Can you guess what the *path* means based on these definitions?

As you may have noticed, all of these words relate to feelings and emotions. They are related to the Greek *pathos*, meaning "feeling," or 'emotion." These words are built by adding prefixes to the root *path*:

- The prefix *sym-* (or *syn-* in many words) means "together," so to **sympathize** with someone is to understand how a friend feels, to relate to their situation, and to be on their side when they're having a hard time.

- The prefix *em-* means "in," so **empathy** refers to emotions that go into you or someone else. Empathy is stronger than sympathy because someone who is empathetic truly feels another person's emotions, rather than just understanding them.

- The prefix *a-* means "without," so someone **apathetic** feels no emotion.

CONTINUED

PEARL
PERL   noun

Pearls are formed inside the shells of living oysters and other mollusks. The word comes from the Latin *perna*, literally meaning "ham," because the shells of the mollusks were shaped like hams.

PECULIAR
puh-KYOOL-yar   adjective

The word "peculiar" can describe an item or trait that is specific to one person or group. It can also describe something that is strange because it is rare or unusual. It comes from the Latin *peculium*, which generally meant "private property" but literally means "property in cattle" because cows were considered the most important form of property and wealth.

PEDESTRIAN
puh-DESS-tree-an   noun

A pedestrian is someone who walks instead of riding in a car or on a bike or horse. It comes from the Latin *pedester*, meaning "on foot." You'll also notice *ped-* in words like "pedometer," a device for counting the number of steps you take in a day.

PEDIGREE
PED-uh-gree   noun

In dog shows, you often hear the word "pedigree" used to describe the genes of the dogs' parents and grandparents. Pedigree was originally a fifteenth-century word for a drawing of a family tree, showing human parents and grandparents. It comes from the Old French phrase *pied de gru*, meaning "the foot of a crane." The name comes from old documents that show family relationships connected by a forked symbol that was shaped like a bird's footprint.

PERFECT   *PUR-fect*   *adjective*

Something that is perfect is totally flawless. It comes from the Latin *perfectus*, meaning "completely made," a combination of *per*, or "completely," and *facere*, "to make or do."

PERFUME   *pur-FYOOM*   *noun*

A perfume is a fragrant oil or spray that is meant to make a person or space smell good. Many perfumes were first made as incense, a material that can be burned to make fragrant smoke fill the room. It's this practice that relates to the word's etymology. Adopted from French, it is formed by the Latin *per-*, meaning "through," and *fumare*, meaning "to smoke."

PERHAPS   *pur-HAPS*   *adverb*

This word literally means "by chance," from the Middle English *per*, meaning "by" or "through," and *hap*, meaning "chance" or "fortune." *Hap* is also the source of "happen" (occurring by chance or fortune) and "happy" (something fortunate that happens to you).

Example: Perhaps you have learned something new from this definition!

PERPLEX   *pur-PLEKS*   *verb*

To be perplexed is to be confused. The word comes from the Latin *perplexus*, also meaning "confused," which was made up of *per-*, or "through," and *plexus*, or "tangled."

PESSIMIST   *PESS-uh-mist*   *noun*

A pessimist is someone who always believes that something bad is going to happen—the opposite of an optimist. It was coined in 1794 from the Latin *pessimus*, meaning "worst." The word was first used to describe the ideas of philosophers who believed that people were not naturally kind.

PHILANTHROPY   *fuh-LAN-thruh-pee*   noun

A philanthropist is someone who regularly volunteers or donates money to those who are less fortunate. Philanthropy comes from the Greek *philanthropos*, meaning "loving mankind," and is formed by *phil-*, or "love," and *anthropos*, or "mankind."

PHILOSOPHY   *fill-AW-soh-fee*   noun

This topic is all about what it means to be alive, aware, and human. It also has to do with studying and building on knowledge of the past. Ancient Greek philosophers, including Plato, Socrates, and Aristotle, created the foundation for Western philosophy, so it's no surprise that the word comes from the Greek *philosophia*, literally meaning "love of knowledge."

PHOTOGRAPH   *FOH-tuh-graff*   noun

This word was created in 1839 by combining the Greek *photo-*, or "light," and *graph*, meaning something used to make a record or write something down. Basically, a photograph uses light to make a record of something. Some of the earliest cameras used plates and materials that were sensitive to light to capture images, with the goal of making visual records of important people and moments.

PHOTOSYNTHESIS *FOH-toh-SIN-thuh-sis*   noun

Photosynthesis is the way plants use light, water, and carbon dioxide to feed themselves and make the oxygen we breathe. The prefix *photo-* is Greek for "light." On its own, "synthesis" is a word for combining things to make a system. In Greek, *synthesis* means "a putting together." So, photosynthesis is the process of putting together light (with other things) to make a system that gives the plant life.

PHYSICS   *FIZ-iks*   *noun*

Physics is the study of how the universe behaves and how things move through space and time. It is a branch of what we call "natural science," which also includes chemistry, geology, and biology. The word "physics" comes from the Greek phrase *ta physika*, meaning "the natural things," from the base word *physis*, or "nature." This is also the source of the word "physical," which describes things related to the body, its nature, and its five senses.

PIONEER   *PIY-uh-neer*   *noun*

We usually think of a pioneer as someone who is the first to set out on an adventure into unexplored territory, but its origin is much simpler. It comes from the Old French *paonier*, meaning "foot-soldier," or a soldier who walks (instead of riding on a horse). Today's definition evolved from the fact that soldiers were often the ones sent out to explore new lands.

PIRATE   *PIY-ret*   *noun/verb*

Pirates are usually thought of as swashbuckling criminals like Blackbeard and Anne Bonny (or Captain Hook and Jack Sparrow in fictional stories). These high-seas bandits were famous and active during the golden age of pirates, which spanned from the 1650s to the 1730s. They would sail up to unsuspecting ships and steal all of the cargo on board. Sometimes they'd steal the whole ship! Pirates get their name from the Greek *peiran*, meaning "to attack."

PLACEBO   *pluh-SEE-boh*   noun

A placebo is made to look exactly like medicine, but it doesn't actually contain medicine in it. Doctors and scientists use placebos to test whether patients are really feeling effects from a medicine or if the effects are in their mind. In Latin, *placebo* means "I shall please." It is connected to today's word because some people who take a placebo think that the fake medicine really works—it literally "pleases" them by making them think they are being cured. This reaction is called a "placebo effect." For many years, it was also a word for someone who showed up to a funeral to get free food but didn't actually know the person who died.

PLAGIARISM   *PLAY-djar-iz-um*   noun

To plagiarize is to copy someone's work and pretend that you created it. It is a form of stealing. It comes from the Latin *plagiare*, meaning "to kidnap."

Example: He copied an essay from the internet, and was kicked out of school for plagiarism.

PLATEAU   *plat-OH*   noun

A plateau is a high, flat piece of land with steep cliffs on its sides. It was adopted directly from the French *plateau*, meaning "table-land," originally from the Greek *platys*, or "flat."

PLATYPUS   *PLAT-uh-puss*   noun

Platypuses are animals most recognizable for their duck-like bills. This feature inspired their other name, the Australian duckmole. But the more common name, platypus, refers to their webbed feet that make them excellent swimmers: The Greek *platypous* means "flat-footed." It is from *platys*, meaning "broad" or "flat," and *pous*, meaning "foot."

POCKET   POK-it   noun
In Old North French, a *poque* was a bag. The ending *-et* or *-ete* is used in some words as a diminutive, or a way of making a word small. So, a "pocket" would be a little *poque*, or a small bag.

POISON   POY-zun   noun/verb
Most poisons in early stories—both historic and fictional—were swallowed in deadly liquid potions and drinks. The Greek philosopher Socrates was famously executed by drinking the poison hemlock. The word comes from the Latin *potare*, meaning "to drink."

POLITE   puh-LITE   adjective
To be polite is to have good manners. It comes from the Latin *politus*, which was used in the same way but literally meant "polished."

PONDER   PAWN-dur   verb
To ponder something is to think about it carefully. "Ponder" first meant "to estimate the worth of," from the Latin *ponderare*, meaning "consider or reflect," just like the modern English word. But its literal meaning was "to weigh," which is why you can think of pondering as weighing something in your mind.

PORCUPINE   PORK-yoo-pine   noun
These animals, which use sharp quills to defend themselves, were formerly called *porke despyne*, from the Old French *porc-espin*, which literally means "spiny pig" or "thorny pig." The French comes from the Latin *porcus*, meaning "hog," and *spina*, meaning "thorn" or "spine."

PORPOISE   *POR-puss*   *noun*

"Porpoise," the name of several species of aquatic mammals closely related to dolphins, literally means "pig-fish," from the Old French *porpais* (made up of *porc*, meaning "pig, swine," and *peis*, meaning "fish"). It's probably a translation of Germanic words like the Old Norse *mar-svin*, meaning "merswine," which was also an early English word for porpoises or small dolphins. As you can probably guess, "merswine," or "sea-pig," is similar to "mermaid," which means "sea-girl."

PRECOCIOUS   *pruh-KOH-shiss*   *adjective*

If you're a precocious student, it means that you understand things quickly and are maybe more mature than expected. It comes from the Latin *praecox*, which first referred to crops and flowers but also meant "ripening before the usual time." In the same way, people who are precocious act more grown up or wiser before the usual time. The Latin word is made up of the elements *prae*, meaning "before," and *coquere*, meaning "to ripen."

PREDATOR   *PREH-duh-tur*   *noun*

Predators are animals that eat other animals for survival. Some predators (carnivores) eat only meat, while others eat both meat and plants (omnivores) or insects (insectivores). The word "predator" comes from the Latin *praedator,* or "robber," from *praeda*, meaning "plunder" or "prey." It was originally used only for insects that eat other insects, but it was later extended to other types of animals.

PREDICT   *pruh-DICT*   *verb*

To predict an event is to think or know it's going to happen before it does. It comes from the Latin *praedicere*, meaning "to foretell," literally "to say before." It is from the elements *prae*, or "before," and *dicere*, or "to say."

PREGNANT   *PREHG-nent*   *adjective*

This word literally means "before birth," from the Latin *prae-*, or "before," and *gnasci,* meaning "to be born." For many years, it was considered impolite to say that a woman was pregnant. Instead, people used phrases like "She's in a family way" or "She's in a delicate condition." It was also common to say that a woman was "with child."

PREJUDICE   *PREH-djuh-diss*   *noun*

Prejudice is dislike for or mistreatment of someone because of something they cannot control. It comes from the Latin *prae-*, or "before," and *iudicium,* meaning "judgment," because prejudice means that you negatively judge someone before you get to know them.

PRETEND   *pruh-TEND*   *verb*

This word's Latin source *praetendere* means "to stretch in front" or "to put forward," just like you stretch your imagination to experience a world different from your own when you pretend to be a superhero or a dragon.

PRINCE/PRINCESS *PRINTS, print-SESS*   *noun*

A prince or princess wasn't always the name for the next person in line for the throne. It was often a ruler in his or her own right, ruling over an area of land called a principality. The word comes from the Latin *princeps,* meaning someone who "takes first" or "grasps first," suggesting that he or she was the most important person in the area.

PRIVILEGE   *PRIH-vuh-ledj*   *noun*

A privilege is a special right given to a person or group that not everyone has. According to Roman law, privilege wasn't always a good thing. The word *privilegium* was made up of the elements *privus*, or "individual,' and *lex*, or law. It meant a law that was created for just one person. However, the law could either benefit that person by allowing them to do something that others couldn't, or it could stop them from doing something that everyone else was allowed to do.

PROBLEM   *PRAWB-lim*   *noun*

A problem is a challenge, or something you have to overcome. Whether you're looking at a math problem or facing a difficult problem that you have to deal with in your day-to-day life, a problem is something that is at the front of your mind until you solve it. This word's Greek origin *proballein* means something "thrown forward," from the prefix *pro-*, meaning "forward," and *ballein* meaning "to throw."

PROCRASTINATE   *pruh-CRASS-tuh-nate*   *verb*

To procrastinate is to put something off until a later time or date. Have you ever procrastinated instead of finishing a big homework assignment, waiting until the last moment to do it? If you break down this word, it means "to put off until tomorrow," from the Latin prefix *pro-*, or "forward," and *crastinus*, or "belonging to tomorrow."

PROTAGONIST   *pruh-TAG-oh-nist*   *noun*

The main character in a story is known as the protagonist. The word comes from the Greek *protagonistes*, which was a word for the main actor in a play. It is made up of the words *protos*, meaning "first," and *agonistes*, meaning "actor" or "competitor."

PROTOTYPE   *PROH-toh-tiyp*   *noun*

When an inventor creates a new machine or device, the first one she makes is called a prototype. The prototype is then used to make more like it. This word comes from the Greek *prototypon*, meaning "a first form." It is made from the Greek *protos*, meaning "first," and *typos*, meaning "pattern" or "mold."

Example: The prototype for the toy car looked so cool! She couldn't wait to test-drive a later model.

PROTRUDE   *proh-TROOD*   *verb*

To protrude is to stick out from something else. For example, your nose protrudes from your face. A blade of grass protrudes from the ground. This word comes from the Latin *protrudere*, meaning "to thrust forward" or "to push out." It comes from the prefix *pro-*, meaning "forward," and *trucere*, meaning "to thrust" or "to push."

PROUD   *PROWD*   *adjective*

When you're feeling proud, you have positive feelings about something you have said or done. It often comes after stretching yourself or trying something new. You might walk with your head held high and your chest forward. You're not afraid of any challenge! This word originally comes from a Proto-Indo-European root meaning "to be forward."

PSEUDONYM   *SOO-doh-nim*   *noun*

A pseudonym is a nickname or a made-up name you use instead of your own. For example, the author Mark Twain, who wrote *The Adventures of Tom Sawyer*, was actually named Samuel Clemens. Mark Twain was his pseudonym! The children's author Judith Sussman used the pseudonym Judy Blume. Many authors use pseudonyms to protect their identity or because they sound more fun or are easier to remember. This word comes from the Greek *pseudonymos*, meaning "having a false name." It is made up of the elements *pseudes*, or "false," and *onoma*, or "name."

PSYCHOLOGY   *SY-kol-oh-jee*   *noun*

Psychology is the study of the human mind and our behavior. In the 1600s, it had a slightly different meaning. It was the study of the human soul or spirit, also known as the "psyche." It is made up of the Greek word *psykhe*, meaning "breath," "soul," or "spirit," and the ending *-logia*, meaning "the study of."

PTERODACTYL

TAIR-oh-DACT-ill

noun

A pterodactyl was a type of flying reptile that lived during the time of the dinosaurs. The bones in their wings were shaped like hands with very long fingers, and the skin stretched between them enabled them to fly, like the wings of a bat. They were named after these wings. The word is made up of the Greek *pteron*, meaning "wing," and *daktylos*, meaning "finger."

PURPLE   *PUR-pull*   *adjective*

Did you know this color is named after a snail? Dye of this color was first made using a gland from a type of snail called *purpura* in Latin. In order to make enough dye to change the color of fabric, thousands of the snails were found and gathered. The snails' shells were cracked and then the tiny gland was removed from each one. As a result, purple clothing was reserved only for royalty and the wealthy who could afford it.

QUEEN

Read more on page 179

Q

QUADRILATERAL   *KWAD-ruh-LAT-ur-ell*   *adjective/noun*

This is another word for a shape that is square or rectangular—any four-sided shape. It comes from the Latin *quadri-*, meaning "four," and *lateris*, meaning "side."

QUAINT   *KWAYNT*   *adjective*

You might call a small, historic town "quaint." It refers to something charming because it is old-fashioned, but its meaning has changed over time. It first meant "proud and clever," a meaning that came from the Latin *cognitus*, or "known." Later, it meant something "skillfully made," which also describes the work of old-fashioned artisans and craftsmen.

Example: The teacups I found at Granny's were so quaint!

QUAKE   *KWAYK*   *noun/verb*

This word means to shudder or shake. Often short for earthquake, this word comes from the Old English *cweccan*, meaning "to cause to shake or tremble."

QUARANTINE   *KWAR-un-teen*   *noun/verb*

Sick people are sometimes confined to a place, quarantined, to avoid getting other people sick. It comes from the Latin word *quadraginta*, meaning "forty." The number has to do with the Black Plague. In the 1300s, ships that sailed to Venice from countries where the plague had spread were required to wait 40 days before entering the port to make sure that no one on board was sick!

QUARREL   *KWAR-ull*   *noun/verb*

If you have siblings, you've probably quarreled, or argued, with them. It comes from the Latin *querella*, meaning "complaint" or "accusation."

QUEEN

KWEEN

noun

This word for a female ruler comes from a Proto-Indo-European root meaning "woman." In casual language, it's used to describe a powerful woman.

QUESTION   *KWES-chun*   *noun/verb*

When you ask a question, you're going on a quest for answers. Both come from the Latin *quaerere*, meaning "to seek," "to ask," or "to gain."

QUICK   *KWIK*   *adjective*

When you move quickly, do you feel more alive? "Quick" comes from the Old English word *cwic*, meaning "living," "alive," or "animated."

QUIET   *KWIY-ut*   *adjective*

This word usually refers to a lack of sound. Originally, it had a broader meaning, describing a general calm or stillness. It comes from the Latin *quies*, meaning "rest" or "peace."

QUIXOTIC   *kwik-SOT-ick*   *adjective*

This word means "idealistic," "unrealistic," or "impractical." It comes from the name of the fictional character Don Quixote de La Mancha, who went off on a comedic and knightly adventure many years after knights and chivalry became outdated. The name "Quixote," or *quijote* in Spanish, means "thigh" or a piece of armor you would wear on your thigh.

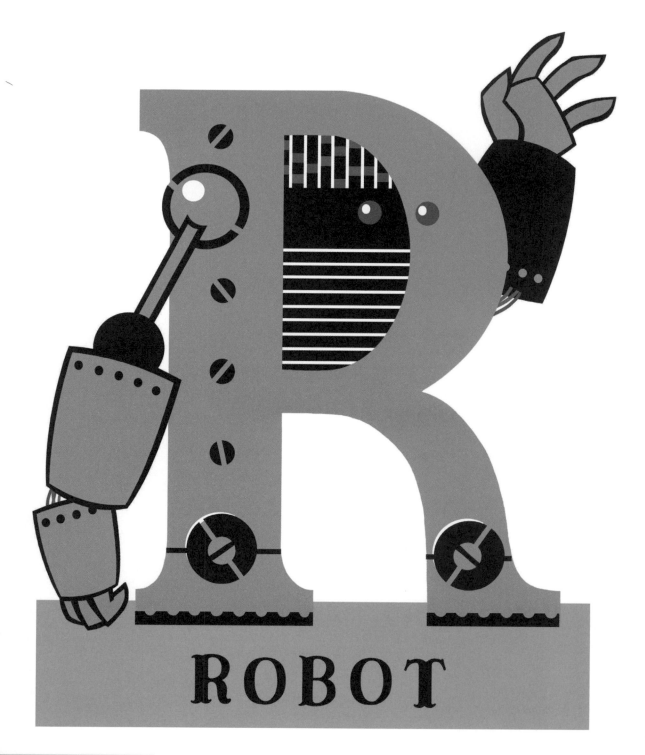

ROBOT

Read more on page 185

R

RACCOON   *RAK-oon*   *noun*

These furry mammals have front paws that are almost as dexterous, or nimble, as human hands, and that's where they get their name. "Raccoon" comes from the Algonquian word *arahkunem*, which means "he scratches with the hands."

RADIATE   *RAY-dee-ayt*   *verb*

To say something "radiates" means that it extends or comes out from a center point, like sunlight shines from the sun. You could also say that the petals of a daisy radiate from the center of the flower because they extend out of it. The origin of this word is the Latin *radius*, which could mean either "a beam of light" or "the spoke of a wheel."

RANDOM   *RAN-dum*   *adjective*

This word originally meant to do something very quickly, and therefore carelessly. It comes from the Old French *randir*, meaning "to run fast." This leads to today's meaning of something that is done without conscious thought, method, or decision.

READ   *REED*   *verb*

Reading can be a good way to learn lessons or get advice. It comes from the Old English *rædan*, which had many meanings but mainly meant "to advise." An adviser is someone who can help you understand something or explain a new idea. Advisers also help put a difficult situation into an order that makes sense—much like a book can.

REBUKE
ree-BYOOK   *verb*

To rebuke someone is to sharply tell them that their actions or words are inappropriate or wrong. The "buke" in "rebuke" comes from a French word meaning "to chop wood," and in that context *re-* means "back." So, the "clapback" of yesteryear was the "chop-back."

RECOGNIZE
REK-egg-niys   *verb*

If you recognize someone, you've probably met them before. This word's Latin source, *recognoscere*, literally means "to get to know [someone or something] again." The Latin is made up of the prefix *re-*, meaning "again," the prefix *co-*, meaning "together," and the base word *gnoscere*, meaning "to know."

RECREATION
REK-ree-ay-shun   *noun*

Recreational activities are those that you do for fun. The prefix *re-* ("again") with *creation* tells you it means "to make or create again." The idea is that activities done just for fun make you happier by restoring you after a long period of hard work. In the fourteenth century, it was also used as a word for "refreshment," as in food and drink to make you feel full and restored after you've been hungry and thirsty.

RECTIFY
REK-tuh-fiy   *verb*

To rectify a problem is to fix it or make it better. It comes from the Latin *rectificare*, meaning "to make right," or literally "to straighten," as you might fix something bent or broken.

REDUNDANT
ruh-DUN-dunt   *adjective*

Something redundant is repetitive. It comes from the Latin *redundare*, meaning "overflowing" or "in excess," formed by *re-*, "again," and *undare*, meaning "to rise in waves."

REFUGE *REF-yooj* noun

This word for a safe place or shelter is made up of the Latin *re-*, "back," *fugere*, "to flee," and the suffix *-ium*, "a place for." Together, it means "a place for fleeing back to." Similarly, a "refugee" is someone who flees to a new place to take shelter.

REJECT *ree-JEKT* verb

To reject something is to not want it, to refuse to accept it. It comes from the Latin *reicare*, meaning "to throw back." It is made up of the prefix *re-*, meaning "back" or "again," and *iacere*, meaning "to throw."

RELIGION *ruh-LIDJ-uhn* noun

Some historians believe that this word comes from the Latin *relegere*, meaning "to read again," suggesting religious study and discussion. Others think it comes from *religare*, meaning "to bind tightly," as in the bond between humans and the gods. In the second case, the prefix *re-* would be an intensifier, added to the base word *ligare*, meaning "to bind."

RELUCTANT *ruh-LUCK-tent* adjective

To be reluctant is to be unwilling to do something. It comes from the Latin *reluctari*, meaning "to struggle against." In this case, the prefix *re-* means "against," and the base word *luctari* means "to struggle" or "to wrestle." This gives "reluctance" the sense of struggling against something you don't want to do.

RENAISSANCE *REN-uh-zaunts* noun

A renaissance is a wave of new ideas and creative works. One famous renaissance happened during the Renaissance era from the fourteenth and seventeenth centuries. Ideas from the ancient Greeks and Romans were used to create new styles of art and music, new inventions and technologies, and new philosophies. The word itself was adopted from French and means "rebirth." The French originally comes from the Latin *renasci*, meaning "to be born again," from the prefix *re-*, "again," and *nasci*, "to be born."

RENEGADE   *REN-uh-gayd*   noun

A renegade is someone who turns against a person, country, or set of ideas. While renegades can be destructive, they can also question the status quo, or the way things have been. In this way, renegades can inspire new ways of thinking or acting. It comes from the same idea as the verb "renege," which means to reject or deny an agreement. Both words come from the Latin *renegare*, meaning "to deny."

Example: He was a renegade for the way he questioned the community center's "no kids allowed" rule.

RESOLVE   *ruh-ZOLV*   verb

To resolve a conflict is to end it by finding middle ground between two people or groups who disagree. This word comes from the Latin prefix *re-*, "again," and *solvere*, "to loosen, release, or explain." It originally meant "to break something down into parts." So, when you resolve a conflict, you're loosening the tension and breaking down the disagreement into manageable parts.

RESPECT   *ree-SPEKT*   noun/verb

To respect someone or have respect for them is to understand and recognize that they are important and deserve to be heard and treated well. It can also mean that you have a very positive opinion of someone and want to be like them. This word comes from the Latin *respicere*, meaning "to look back at" or "to consider." It is from *re-*, meaning "back" or "often," and *specere*, meaning "to look at." The prefix suggests that you look closely at people you find important.

RHETORIC   *REHT-ur-ik*   noun

Rhetoric is the art of writing or speaking in a way that persuades people to agree with you. It comes from the Greek *rhetorike tekhne*, meaning "the art of an orator" or public speaker. *Rhetor* was a word for a master of public speaking in Ancient Greece.

RHINOCEROS   riy-NOSS-ur-uss   noun

The name of this large, horned animal comes from its most distinctive feature. The Greek *rhinos* means "nose," and *keras* means "horn."

RHYME   RIYME   noun

> *Hickory dickory dock*
>
> *the mouse ran up the clock*

These famous lines rhyme because the last syllable in each line sounds the same. Rhymes can give stories, poems, and songs a musical or flowing quality. The word comes from the Greek *rhythmos*, which meant "measured flow or movement," or "symmetry."

RIDICULOUS   rih-DIK-yoo-luss   adjective

Something that is ridiculous is so absurd, strange, or unexpected that it's funny. It comes from the Latin *ridere*, meaning "to laugh."

ROBOT

POH-bot

noun

This word comes from the Czech word *robotnik*, meaning "forced worker." It first appeared in a 1920 science fiction play called *R.U.R. or "Rossum's Universal Robots,"* by Czech writer Karel Čapek. His brother Josef invented this word as a name for the artificial characters in the play. Today we use "robot" as a word for a machine created to do a task independently.

RODENT   *ROH-dent*   *noun*

Rats, mice, hamsters, and squirrels are all examples of rodents. Their name comes from the Latin *rodere*, meaning "to gnaw," because rodents are known for their large front teeth designed for nibbling away at things.

ROMANCE   *ROH-manss*   *noun*

We usually associate this word with love and relationships, but this wasn't always the case. It was originally a word for any story told "in the Roman style," or *romanz* in Old French. The Roman style would have originally been in a poem. Over time, it came to mean any story told in everyday language, not something legal or political. Stories told in this casual style were usually adventure stories about knights and chivalry. These stories often featured a love story, and love took over as the primary meaning.

ROYALTY   *ROY-ul-tee*   *noun*

Kings, queens, princes, and princesses are all considered royalty. This word comes from the Latin *regalis*, meaning "kingly" or "like a king." *Regalis* itself comes from a Proto-Indo-European root meaning "to move in a straight line."

RUCKUS   *RUK-uss*   *noun*

This word represents a great hullabaloo or chaos! It is a blend of "rumpus" and the old word "ruction," which means "disturbance." "Rumpus" might come from a Latin word meaning "to break," or it might be a variation of "robustious," a seventeenth-century English word for "noisy" or "robust."

Example: The fireworks in the neighborhood caused quite the ruckus on the block!

RUMOR   *ROO-mur*   *noun*

It's not kind to spread rumors, especially if you know they aren't true. This word comes from the Latin *rumorem*, meaning "noise" or "clamor." It refers to talk of "common people" who spread news by word of mouth.

SARCOPHAGUS

Read more on page 189

S

SABOTAGE   *SAB-oh-taj*   verb

To sabotage a plan is to mess it up on purpose. It comes from the French *saboter*, which means to "bungle" or to goof something up. It is based on the word *sabot*, or "wooden shoe," so it literally means to walk noisily and clumsily as if wearing wooden shoes. Some stories suggest that the meaning evolved because workers would throw their shoes into machinery to protest poor treatment.

SAFARI   *suh-FAR-ee*   noun

A safari is a word for a trip to see wildlife in their natural habitat. It's common for people to "go on safari" in East Africa. The word is borrowed from Swahili and means "journey."

SALMON   *SAM-un*   noun

These fish are known for their unique migration habits. They swim upstream against the current, leaping out of the water to make their way to the place where they mate. The word's origin isn't entirely certain, but it probably means "leaper," from the Latin *salire*, "to leap."

SAMURAI   *SAM-ur-iy*   noun

A samurai was a noble military officer in medieval and historic Japan. It is borrowed from Japanese and means "knight" or "warrior."

SANCTUARY   *SANK-choo-airy*   noun

This word refers to any building or hall for religious worship, like a temple or a cathedral. The Late Latin *sanctarium* meant "sacred place" or "shrine." It is originally from the Latin *sanctus*, or "holy." This is the same source as the word "saint."

SARCASTIC   SAR-cass-tik   adjective

To be sarcastic is to say something that you obviously don't mean in an insulting or mocking way. "Sarcastic" comes from the Greek *sarka-zein*, literally "to strip off the flesh," from *sarx*, meaning "flesh." The idea is that sarcasm is cutting or biting humor that reveals the intention "beneath the skin," or beneath the literal meaning of the words.

SARCOPHAGUS

sar-KOFF-uh-guss

noun

A sarcophagus is a stone coffin that was commonly used in Egyptian, Greek, and Roman cultures. It comes from the name of the limestone that was often used to make the coffins, the Greek *sarkophagos*, literally meaning "flesh-eating" because it was thought that limestone could dissolve dead bodies. The Greek word is made up of the elements *sarx*, meaning "flesh," and *phagein*, meaning "to eat."

SCANDAL   SKAN-dull   noun

A scandal is when someone, usually a prominent person, does something that most people think is bad or immoral. A scandal usually causes the person to become unpopular, and they sometimes lose their job. It comes from the Greek *skandalon*, meaning "stumbling block."

SCAVENGER   *SKAV-en-jur*   noun

If you've ever been on a scavenger hunt, you know that you have to search an area for small items, based on a set of clues that lead you from one place to the next. It's a fun game! But the original act of scavenging wasn't so fun. Before toilets were common in every house and garbage trucks picked up trash, people threw all of the things—and bodily waste—they wanted to throw away into the gutter, a trench beside the street. A scavenger was a person who was hired to look for garbage and waste on the street and clean it up. A scavenger is also a type of animal that eats what other animals leave behind. The word originally comes from the Old English *sceawian*, meaning "to look at" or "to inspect."

SCUTTLEBUTT   *SKUT-ul-but*   noun

This word means "office chatter" or "gossip." It was first a sailor's term for a cask (called a "butt," from the Old English *buttuc*, or "end") of drinking water with a hole in it for getting to the water (called a "scuttle," from the Spanish *escotar*, meaning "cut out"). The word's meaning changed to "rumor" or "gossip" because sailors would gather to chat around the cask, just as office workers do around a watercooler.

SEASON   *SEE-zon*   noun

Paying attention to the change in seasons is very important for people who grow crops. In ancient times, people's survival depended upon crops growing well. The word originally comes from the Latin *serere*, meaning "to sow," another word for planting seeds.

SECRETARY   *SEK-ruh-tarry*   noun

A secretary is someone who manages the records and meetings of a company or businessperson. In the fourteenth century, a secretary was literally someone who was trusted to keep secrets. This word and "secret" both come from the Latin *secretus*, meaning "hidden" or "private."

SENSITIVE   *SEN-suh-tiv*   *adjective*

The skin on your fingers is sensitive: With your fingertips, you can feel textures and temperatures better than you can with other parts of your body. And someone with a sensitive personality feels emotions more than other people do. This word comes from the Old French *sensitif*, and before that the Latin *sensitivus*, both meaning "capable of feeling." The base Latin word *sentire* means "to feel" or "to perceive."

SENTENCE   *SEN-tints*   *noun/verb*

In law and legal situations, a sentence is the decision of a judge or a ruler. For example, someone who has committed a crime may be sentenced to go to prison. In grammar, a sentence is a complete thought with a subject and a predicate. For example, this is a complete sentence: "The dog barked." The original Latin word *sententia* was more connected to the legal term. The base word *sentire* means "to feel" or "to perceive" and reflects the idea of a person making a decision, having an opinion, and passing judgment. But the legal sense also led to the grammatical sense: When a judge passes a sentence, that decision is complete and final, just like a complete sentence.

SEQUIN   *SEE-kwin*   *noun*

Sequins are often added to clothing to make them shimmer and sparkle. The Arabic *sikka* was a word for a minting die, or a special stamp used for making coins. The name of a sequin comes from this Arabic word thanks to its resemblance to a tiny, shiny coin.

SEQUOIA   *suh-KOY-ah*   *noun*

A sequoia is a huge species of tree named after the Cherokee man Sequoyah (also spelled Sikwayi). In the 1800s, he invented a writing system for the Cherokee language, making reading and writing possible for the people who spoke the language. The invention increased literacy so much that a greater percentage of Cherokee people could read and write than European Americans at the time.

SHAMPOO   *SHAM-poo*   *noun*

This word comes from the Hindi word *champna*, meaning "to massage" or "to knead the muscles." In the 1800s, it was extended to the massaging motion you use to wash your hair, and later came to refer to the soap made for use in hair.

SHERBET   *SHUR-bet*   *noun*

This type of icy treat is similar to a fruity ice cream. It was originally a word for a drink made of fruit juice and sweet water that was popular in the Middle East and other surrounding regions, named from the Arabic *shariba*, meaning "to drink."

SHERIFF   *SHARE-uff*   *noun*

A sheriff was called a *scirgerefa* in Old English. This word is made up of *scir*, a word for a shire, meaning a county or area, and *gerefa*, meaning a "chief" or "official." So, a sheriff is a chief or official who oversees a shire or county.

SHIVER   *SHIV-ur*   *verb*

The word "shiver" originally referred to a small piece or splinter of something, or the act of breaking something into many small pieces. When pirates say "Shiver me timbers," they're talking about the splintering of their wooden ships during battles on the rough seas. This word comes from a Proto-Germanic root meaning "split." However, when you shiver from the cold, you're using a word with a completely different origin. It was originally spelled *chiveren* and most likely comes from the Old English word *ceafl*, or "jaw," because your jaw shakes when you're cold, making your teeth chatter!

SHUTTLE SHUT-ull noun

The most notable types of shuttles we use today are space shuttles that go back and forth between the earth and space. We also call buses and trains that run back and forth between two locations "shuttles." In Old English, a *scytel* was a dart or an arrow, which also shoots into the sky and certainly looks like a space shuttle. However, the modern word might be named after a certain weaving tool that was "shot" back and forth across the threads, just like a train, bus, or space shuttle.

SIDEBURNS SIYD-burnz noun

This beard style features whiskers on the side of a man's face. These can lead into a mustache, but the chin is always shaven. The style was named after the American Civil War general Ambrose E. Burnside, who had sideburns and a mustache that were so big and bushy that he made the style especially popular.

SIGNIFICANT sig-NIF-uh-kant adjective

Something that is significant has value or points to an outcome. It comes from the Latin *significare*, meaning "to make (something) known" or "to point (something) out." This is based on the Latin *signum*, meaning "sign," and *facere*, meaning "to make." The Romans believed that natural things like flocks of birds and lunar eclipses were signs that something important was about to happen.

Example: After practicing every day, he made significant improvement on playing the guitar.

SIREN SIY-run noun

A siren (originally from the Greek *Seiren*) is a mythical nymph or spirit who looks like a woman. She sings a beautiful, irresistible song to call sailors so that she can drown them. The other meaning of "siren," a loud warning sound, comes from the name of this mythical creature.

SKELETON   *SKEL-it-un*   *noun*

After we die, our bones can last many centuries. Over time, the moisture evaporates from bones, leaving them white. The Greek *skeletos* means "dried-up" and was used to describe mummies as they decayed.

SKEPTICAL   *SKEP-tick-ull*   *noun*

If you're skeptical about something your friend has told you, it means that you doubt it is true. The word comes from the Greek *skeptikos*, meaning "inquiring" and "reflective." There was a group of Greek philosophers called the Skeptics who preferred to question and reflect on everything, rather than accepting it immediately. If you like to fact-check everything you hear or read, you probably think like the Skeptics!

Example: My brother told me he didn't eat the last slice of pizza, but I am skeptical.

SKETCH   *SKETCH*   *noun*

A sketch is a light drawing, usually in pencil, that is not as detailed as a finished piece of artwork. The word may be from the Greek *skhedios*, meaning "temporary" or "offhand."

SLANG   *SLANG*   *noun*

While the etymology of "slang" isn't known for certain, it is thought to come from the Norwegian phrase *slengja kjeften*, which literally meant "to sling the jaw." It used to mean "to abuse with words," or to insult. The current meaning of "slang" came around in the early 1800s as a name for the casual language of wanderers.

SLEUTH   *SLOOTH*   *noun/verb*

This word is another name for a detective or the act of following clues to solve a mystery. In the thirteenth century, though, it was a word for the trail that was being followed. It is a shortening of the term "sleuth-hound," a type of dog used for tracking and hunting. It comes from the Old Norse *sloð*, meaning "trail."

SLOTH   *SLAWTH*   *noun*

Many cultures consider "sloth," or sluggishness, to be a negative quality. The word comes from the Middle English *slou,* meaning "slow." In the 1600s, this word became the name of an animal as well—an animal that moves so slowly that they're named after their slowness!

SMORGASBORD   *SMORE-gus-bord*   *noun*

A smorgasbord is a buffet with many different types of food. It was adopted from the Swedish *smörgåsbord* and literally means "butter-goose table." *Smör,* or "butter," shares a root with the English "smear," while *gås* comes from the same root as "goose." *Bord* means "table."

SOCIETY   *soh-SIY-it-ee*   *noun*

A society is a group of people who live together or share common interests. Societies can be big or small. You could be part of a Book Lovers' Society that enjoys reading. Or, you could be part of a local, national, or global society that unites people by the way they act or think or by the territory they share. The word was adopted from Old French, but its Latin source is *socius,* meaning "companion" or "ally."

Example: American society values life, liberty, and the pursuit of happiness.

SOLITUDE   *SAWL-i-tood*   *noun*

Solitude is the state of being alone. This word comes from the Latin *solitarius,* meaning "lonely" or away from other people, originally from *solus,* meaning "alone."

SOPHOMORE   *SOFF-more*   *noun*

A sophomore is someone in their second year of college or high school. It comes from the idea of sophism, a style of clever argument that involves trickery. The term is originally from Greek *sophisma*, meaning "clever device" or "stage-trick." This gives "sophomore" the literal meaning "arguer." Do you know any sophomores who, no longer freshmen, are brave enough to make new arguments and assert themselves?

SORCERY   *SOR-sur-ree*   *noun*

Sorcery is the practice of doing magic, as a wizard, witch, or sorcerer does in a fantasy story. Its Latin source, *sortiarius*, was a word for a person who could do magic, but it could also mean fortune-teller. It literally meant "one who influences fate or fortune," from the Latin *sors*, meaning "fate" or "fortune."

ORIGIN SPOTLIGHT: *SPECERE*

The Latin *specere* means "to look at." Adding prefixes, suffixes, and other word elements to this root gives us many different English words that all relate to looking, seeing, and watching. Explore this list of words including *specere*. See if you can think of any others that aren't here!

INSPECT: to look closely at something. By adding the prefix *in-* ("in, on") to *specere*, you get someone looking closely into something.

EXPECT: to know or think that something is going to happen. By adding the prefix *ex-* ("out") to *specere*, you get the idea of someone looking out for something.

SPECTACLE: an amazing sight to see, from the Latin *spectaculum*, meaning "a public show." The base word *spectare*, meaning "to view or watch," is a form of *specere* that suggests a lot of people watching, or something people want to watch again and again.

SPECTATOR: someone who watches a show or performance. The -or ending makes this word into someone who might come to see a spectacle.

RETROSPECT: used in the phrase "in retrospect" to mean "in hindsight" or "thinking back on." Adding the element *retro-*, meaning "backward," to *specere* gives this word the sense of looking backward in time to see your past actions in a new way.

SPONTANEOUS   *SPAWN-tayn-ee-us*   adjective

Suppose your friend suddenly started squawking like a bird and flapping their arms for no reason. That would be pretty spontaneous behavior. Something that happens spontaneously occurs with no warning. It comes from the Latin *spontaneus*, meaning "of one's own free will," and not caused by anyone or anything else.

Example: She is a natural comedian who spontaneously makes jokes.

SQUIRREL   *SKWER-rel*   noun

The name of these agile rodents comes from the Greek word *skiouros*, which means "shadow-tailed." It's formed by the words *skia*, or "shadow," and *oura*, or "tail." Squirrels were likely given this name because they have lightweight tails that follow them like shadows, or maybe because they sometimes hold their long, fluffy tails over their heads to shade themselves from the sun.

STAUNCH   *STAWNCH*   adjective

Someone who is staunch is loyal, committed, and firm in their attitude. For example, you might staunchly believe that lying is always wrong. This word comes from the Latin *stare*, meaning "to stand," because a staunch believer won't budge once they've made up their mind.

Example: He was a staunch advocate for more public libraries.

STEREOTYPE   *STAIR-ee-oh-tiyp*   noun

A stereotype is something people might believe to be true about someone else, but it is often false or overly simple. For example, the idea that all girls like the color pink is a stereotype. Girls might like the color pink, but it isn't a given just because they are a girl. (Boys can like pink, too!) Stereotypes can be dangerous because they don't leave room for individuality. They can also very easily turn into a prejudice. The word "stereotype" was originally a term for a printing plate or stamp that could be used to make many identical copies of an image. Just like a stamped image, the stereotypes about people (and animals!) make them seem like they're all the same. This word is made up of the Greek words *stereos*, meaning "solid," and *typos*, meaning "image" or "stamped impression."

Example: It was a false stereotype that all police officers like doughnuts.

STRATEGY   *STRAT-uh-jee*   noun

In order to win a game or a battle, you need a good strategy. This word comes from the Greek *strategia*, which is made up of *stratos*, a word for "army" (literally meaning "something that is spread out"), and *agos*, meaning "leader." So *strategia* was the leader, or general, spreading out an army across the battlefield in a way that would help them be victorious.

Example: I need a good strategy to beat my dad in chess.

SUBMARINE   *SUB-muh-reen*   noun/adjective

This word literally means "under the sea," from the Latin *sub*, meaning "under" or "below," and *mare*, meaning "sea." In English, it was first an adjective describing things that are under the surface of the ocean (and it can still be used in this way). In the late 1800s, it became a noun for a "submarine boat" or a ship that can travel underwater.

SUCCEED   suck-SEED   *verb*

To succeed is to accomplish your goals. It can also mean "follow," as in "The queen was succeeded by her daughter, the princess." In this case, the princess became queen after her mother. The word comes from the Latin *succedere*, meaning "to come after" or "rise up, ascend." The idea that the princess had a higher rank once she became queen gave us the idea of success, or an achievement.

SUPERIOR   soo-PEER-ee-or   *adjective*

Something that is superior is better or higher quality than other things like it. It comes from the Latin *superiorem*, meaning "higher," from the base word *super*, meaning "above" or "over."

SUPERSONIC   SOO-pur-SAWN-ick   *adjective*

Some superheroes (and even some jets and other very fast vehicles) can travel faster than the speed of sound! That's what this word means. *Super* is a Latin prefix meaning "above" or "beyond," and sonic comes from the Latin *sonus*, meaning "sound."

Example: Lightning is supersonic. That's why you hear the crack of thunder after you see the flash!

SURGEON   SURJ-un   *noun*

Before scientific developments helped us better understand the human body, healers were sometimes thought to have mystical powers. It was a new and exciting development when doctors were able to heal people through surgery, or physically opening their bodies to cure injuries and illnesses. Someone who did this type of procedure was called a "surgeon," from the Greek *kheirourgos*. The word means healing "done by (human) hand," versus healing through the gods or other mystical powers. The Greek is made up of the elements *kheir*, or "hand," and *ergon*, meaning "work."

SURVIVE   SUR-viyv   verb

If you've ever gone to summer camp or grew up exploring the outdoors, you may have learned how to survive in the wild! Survival skills can include how to start a fire, build a shelter, and find food in the wilderness. You can also survive an illness or any other dangerous situation. The word "survive" comes from the Latin *supervivere*, meaning "to live longer than," formed by *super*, "beyond," and *vivere*, "to live." You could say that, literally, superheroes can survive anything!

Example: My friend was in a bike accident, but she survived and is doing well!

SWANKY   SWANK-ee   adjective

A swanky event is one that is very fancy and glamorous. This word became popular in the early 1800s. "Swank" first meant "to strut" or swagger, and later "swanky" described people who might walk in this way, especially if they looked very stylish or posh. It probably comes from a Proto-Germanic root meaning "to swing," as you might swing your arms or hips while walking confidently.

Example: His grandfather threw a very swanky 100th birthday party. They even served apple juice in champagne flutes!

SWORD   SORD   noun

The word "sword" is ancient. It has barely changed from its original Old English spelling, *sweord*. Its older Germanic root means "to cut or pierce."

SYLLABLE   SILL-i-bal   noun

A syllable is a part of a word that makes a single sound when you pronounce it. For example, the word "gibberish" has three syllables: gib-ber-ish. Syllable is derived from the Greek *syllabe*, meaning something that is "held together," just like the syllables are held together by the word.

SYMMETRY *SIM-met-ree* noun

Symmetry is when a shape can be divided down the middle into two identical halves, equal in size and shape. For example, a square split down the middle will create two equally sized rectangles, and a perfect circle split down the middle creates two identical half circles. Many things in nature (including our bodies!) are more or less symmetrical. This word is from the Greek *symmetros*, meaning something of an equal measure. It comes from *syn-*, or "together," and *metron*, or "measure."

PREFIX SPOTLIGHT: *SYN-*

Review the definition of these three words that include the Greek *syn-* as a prefix.

- **SYNONYM:** a word that means the same thing as another word

- **SYNCHRONIZE:** to do something at the same time as someone else

- **SYNERGY:** working together, cooperation

What do they have in common? Can you guess what *syn* means based on these definitions?

Syn means "together" or "same." Synonyms are different words that *name* the *same* thing (from *onoma*, or "name"). **Synchronized** swimmers perform their moves *together* at the *same time* (from *khronos*, or "time"). When classrooms encourage **synergy**, everyone *works together* and gets more done (from *ergon*, or "work").

This prefix is also sometimes spelled *sym* and appears in words like "symmetry" (two halves that are the same), "symphony" (sounds played together), and "symbiosis" (when two kinds of animals live in the same habitat and help each other).

SYNONYM   *SIN-oh-nim*   *noun*

A synonym is a word that has the same meaning as another. For example, "happy," "elated," "delighted," and "pleased" are all synonyms. It comes from the Greek *synonymon*, which is formed by *syn-*, meaning "same," and *onoma*, meaning "name."

TULIP

Read more on page 211

T

TATTOO   *TAT-too*   *noun*

Before you get a tattoo, you should make sure that you really want to have that design on you for the rest of your life. Otherwise, stick to temporary tattoos. In several languages spoken in the Polynesian islands, *tatau* or *tatu* means "puncture" or "a mark made on the skin." It was borrowed by European sailors on expeditions to explore the islands in the 1700s. Tattoos were sometimes used to punish sailors before they became popular fashion statements.

Example: She has a tattoo of a rose on her arm because her mother's name is Rose.

TAXI   *TAK-see*   *noun*

This name for a cab comes from the full phrase "taximeter cab." Taximeter was the original name of the device that taxis used to measure distance and fare (the amount you owe). The word itself comes from "tax," just like the taxes your parents pay. It was adopted directly from the Latin *tax*.

TEACH   *TEECH*   *verb*

To teach is to help someone master new skills, learn new information, and come up with new ideas. This word comes from the Old English *tæcan*, which was usually used to mean "to show," "to warn," or "to persuade." In Old English, it was more common to use the word *læran*, which is also the source of "learn," to mean "teach" or "instruct."

TECHNOLOGY   *TEK-naw-luh-jee*   *noun*

We usually think of art and technology as two separate things—but history tells us they're related! In Greek culture, technology was a term to discuss artistic skills. The base *tekhne* was a word for "art, craft," or a method of making something. So, *Tekhnologia* was literally "the study of making art." The meaning changed from discussing the inner workings of art to the details of "industrial arts," or new machines. It finally came to refer to the inventions themselves.

TELEPHONE   *TELL-uh-fohn*   *noun*

The telephone as we know it was invented in 1849. The word comes from the French *téléphone*, meaning "far sound." *Tele* is Greek for "far off" and appears in words like teleport (to be instantly transported far away), television (a device allowing you to view things happening far away), and telekenesis (to be able to move faraway things with your mind).

TELESCOPE   *TELL-uh-skohp*   *noun*

A telescope can be used to see across long distances over land and sea, or deep into space. The word comes from the Greek *teleskopos*, "far-seeing," which is made up of *tele-*, "far," and *skopos*, or "watcher."

TEMPORARY   *TEM-pur-air-ee*   *adjective*

Something temporary is not here to stay. This word comes from the Latin *temporarius*, meaning "seasonal" or "only lasting a short time." It is originally from the Latin *tempus*, meaning "time" or "season."

TENACITY   *ten-ass-i-tee*   *noun*

When someone has tenacity, it means they are very determined and won't ever give up. This word comes from the Latin *tenacis*, meaning "holding fast," "gripping," or "firm," from *tenere*, meaning "to hold." When you're tenacious, you hold tightly on to your goal until you achieve it—even if it ends up looking different in the end.

Example: He had great tenacity when training for the basketball finals.

TERRARIUM   *tur-AIR-ee-um*   *noun*

A terrarium is a decorative glass container with plants and soil. It gets its name from the Latin *terra*, meaning "earth" or "land." This Latin base word appears in "territory," which means land belonging to a particular area or people. You can also find it in "terrier," or "earth dog," a type of dogs that dig and chase animals into their burrows.

TERRIFIC   *tur-IFF-ik*   *adjective*

Today, we think of something that is "terrific" as a good thing, but that wasn't always the case. This word originally meant the same thing as "terrifying" and "terrible." These things that signaled terror are from the Latin *terrere*, meaning "to fill with fear." The meaning of "terrific" changed in the late 1800s when it was used as a term for something so exciting and fun that it made your heart race.

THERAPY   *THAIR-uh-pee*   *noun*

Different kinds of therapy can be used to treat different illnesses, both physical and mental. It comes from the Greek *therapeutein*, meaning "to cure." The original base word was *therapon*, which meant an attendant, or someone who might look after you when you're sick.

THERMOSTAT   *THERM-oh-stat*   noun

You may have a thermostat on the wall that you can adjust to change the temperature in your home. The earliest thermostats were used in the 1800s to help keep factory machines at the right temperature. The first part comes from the Greek *thermos*, meaning "hot," and the second part comes from *statos*, meaning "standing." Together they create the idea of keeping something standing, or staying, at the same level of heat.

THESAURUS   *thuh-SAWR-us*   noun

A thesaurus is a book full of synonyms and antonyms. Synonyms are words that have the same or similar meanings, like "smart" and "clever." Antonyms are words that have opposite meanings like "hot" and "cold." In Latin, the word *thesaurus* means "a treasure," "a treasure trove," or "a treasury" (a place where you keep and count money). The Latin word comes from the Greek *thesauros*, also a word for "treasury," or a chest where treasure is stored. The idea is that a thesaurus is a treasure trove of words.

THRILL   *THRILL*   noun

Have you ever felt your stomach drop on a roller coaster or been so excited that you couldn't sit still during an action-packed movie? These experiences are "thrills" that make you feel delight, excitement, and even a little bit of fear. This term comes from the Old English *þyrlian*, meaning to pierce a hole in something. The modern meaning of the word comes from the idea of being "pierced with emotion."

TORNADO   *TORN-ay-doh*   noun

The name of this funnel-shaped storm comes from the Latin *tonare*, meaning "to thunder." It is influenced by the Spanish *tornar*, meaning "to twist" or "to turn."

TOURNAMENT   *TORN-uh-mint*   *noun*

Today, a tournament can be any big game or contest between two teams or contenders. But did you know that the earliest ones were all about war games? Tournaments, or tourneys, were medieval contests that allowed knights to show off their skills with battles like jousting. In fact, the word comes from the Old French *tornoier*, meaning "to joust," literally meaning "to turn around." The "turning" possibly comes from the fact that the sport of jousting involved a rider turning a horse around to charge at an opponent and strike them off their horse, or from the sense of "turning" a battle in your favor. The Old French word comes from the Latin *tornare*, meaning "to turn."

TOXIC   *TAWK-sik*   *adjective*

You definitely don't want to eat something toxic—that means it's poisonous. This word comes from the Greek *toxikon*, meaning "related to archery or bows and arrows." It's from *toxon*, or "bow" (as in a bow and arrow). The link between archery and "toxic" comes from the common practice in war of adding poison to the heads of arrows. In Ancient Greek, the phrase *toxikon pharmakon* meant "a poison or drug for arrows." Even though *pharmakon* was the word for "poison" or "drug," the meaning of the full phrase blended over time. *Pharmakon* was dropped, leaving just *toxikon*, or "toxic."

TRAITOR   *TRAY-tur*   *noun*

A traitor is someone who turns against his or her friends. One of the most famous cases of this in history was when a group of Roman senators plotted to kill the ruler Julius Caesar. One of them, Brutus, was Caesar's friend, and according to some stories about the event, Caesar asked in surprise, "*Et tu, Brute?*" This means "And you, Brutus?" The word "traitor" is from the Latin *trans-*, or "over," and *dare,* or "to give." Combined, the word means "to hand over or deliver (someone or something to an enemy)."

TRAJECTORY   *truh-JECT-or-ee*   noun

If you throw a ball to your friend, the ball's trajectory is its path through the air from you to your friend. If you see a shooting star in the night sky, its trajectory is its path as it flies through space and into Earth's atmosphere. The word comes from the Latin *traiectus*, meaning "thrown over" or "thrown across," just like your ball. It is a combination of the Latin word *trans*, meaning "across" or "beyond," and *iacere*, meaning "to throw."

TRANSMIT   *tranz-MIT*   verb

To transmit information is to send it somewhere, usually across a long distance. This word comes from the Latin *transmittere*, meaning "to throw or send across," from the elements *trans*, meaning "across" or "beyond," and *mittere*, meaning "to send" or "to throw."

TRANSPARENT   *tranz-PAIR-ant*   adjective

Something transparent is clear—you can see right through it, like the glass in your window or pure water. It is formed of the two Latin elements *trans*, meaning "through" or "across," and *parare*, meaning "to appear" or "to perceive."

TRANSPORTATION   *TRANZ-por-TAY-shun*   noun

Transportation refers to a way to get people or goods from one place to another. Different modes of transportation include bicycles, cars, trains, boats, and airplanes. It originally comes from the Latin *transportare*, meaning "to carry over" or "to take across." It is made up of the elements *trans*, meaning "beyond" or "across," and *portare*, meaning "to carry."

TREMENDOUS   *truh-MEND-us*   adjective

We usually use this word to mean "very large in size." But in the 1600s, it was a word for something so terrible and awful that it would make you shake in fear! It originates from the Latin *tremere*, "to tremble."

TRIUMPH TRY-umf noun/verb

Today we think of triumph as an act of victory, perhaps defeating an enemy army or a big achievement. The origin of this word, the Latin *triumphus*, was sometimes used in the same way. But it was also a name for an event that happened after the fighting was done. When the general or admiral led the army back home after winning a battle, there was a great procession and parade—a triumph—with music and celebration. The Arc de Triomphe (or "Arch of Triumph") in Paris, France, was made in honor of all of the men and women who fought and died in battle for France.

TRIVIA TRIV-ee-uh noun

This word was coined in 1932 by the author Logan Pearsall Smith, whose book *Trivia* was full of short stories and sayings about everyday life. Today's meaning of "trivia" comes from the book in the sense that it involves knowing tidbits of knowledge. The title was a short version of "trivialities," or small, common things that don't matter much. Its origin is the Latin *trivium*, meaning "a place where three roads meet." Such a place was a public area where anyone could stop and talk. Over time, this came to describe any common area, a place where people met and exchanged facts.

TROLL TROHL noun

Trolls first appeared in Scandinavian mythology, as did the word itself. Although "troll" has been associated with these giant, clumsy monsters for centuries, the word is probably originally derived from a word for "bewitch" or "charm."

TROPHY TROH-fee noun

Have you ever won a trophy for playing on a team or winning a tournament? It comes from the Latin *trophaeum*, a term used in war to mean "a sign of victory." It is originally from the Greek *tropaios*, "of (an enemy's) defeat."

TULIP

TOO-lup

noun

This type of flower is named after the Turkish *tülbent*, meaning "turban," because their big, bright petals are shaped like a tall, colorful Turkish turban, or headwrap.

TURBULENT

TURB-yoo-lint   *adjective*

If you've ever flown somewhere in a plane, you may have heard this word from the pilot when the plane flew through cloudy weather or rough winds. The plane feels like it's running over a bumpy road. Turbulent can also mean "disorderly" or "full of commotion" when talking about a rowdy group of people. This is the older meaning, from the Latin *turba*, meaning "turmoil" or "crowd."

TURTLE

TUR-tull   *noun*

"Turtle" arose around 1600 as a variation of the French word(s) for the animals, *tortue* or *tortre*. Evidently English sailors mutilated the pronunciation of the French so often that it became its own word. Tortoise may be from the Latin *tartaruchus*, meaning "of the underworld."

TUXEDO

TUK-see-doh   *noun*

The formal suit called a tuxedo gets its name from Tuxedo Park in New York. This was once a posh getaway for wealthy city folk who would put on their best clothes to visit the country club there. The word originally comes from an Algonquian word, probably one meaning "crooked river."

TYRANNOSAURUS REX *tiy-RAN-no-sore-us REKS* *noun*

Meet the meaning behind the apex predator! Fossils of these creatures were first found in Wyoming and Montana in the early 1900s, when scientists looked to the Greeks to give the animal a name. The name was built from three words: *tyrannos*, meaning a tyrant (a cruel, powerful ruler); *-saurus,* an ending used for dinosaurs, meaning "lizard"; and *rex*, which is Latin word for "king." Together, the T. rex is literally a "king tyrant lizard."

UNICORN

Read more on page 215

U

UKULELE   *YOU-kuh-lay-lee*   *noun*

A ukulele is a small, guitar-shaped instrument known for its use in Hawaiian music. The Hawaiian *'ukulele* means "leaping flea" because of the quick movements your fingers make when playing it.

ULTIMATE   *OHL-tuh-mit*   *adjective*

Something ultimate is the best, most extreme, or most impressive. It is something that comes at the farthest end of a distance or spectrum. The word originates from the Latin *ultimus*, meaning "last" or "farthest."

UMBRELLA   *um-BRELL-uh*   *noun*

Umbrellas were primarily used as sunshades until people invented water-repellent fabrics for protecting themselves from the rain. In Latin, *umbrella* literally meant "little shadow" or "little shade," from the Latin *umbra*, meaning "shadow" or "shade."

UMPIRE   *UM-piyer*   *noun*

An umpire is an official who supervises some sports, like baseball, and makes decisions when a play is unclear or undecided. In baseball, the umpire calls whether the pitch is a "strike" or a "ball," and if the ball is "fair" or "foul." This word comes from the Latin *nonper*, meaning "odd number," because an umpire is a third person who settles arguments and makes fair calls. The first umpires acted as referees in wrestling matches.

UNANIMOUS   *YOU-nan-uh-mus*   *adjective*

If you and your friends make a unanimous decision, you all agree on the same thing. This word comes from the Latin *unanimus*, meaning "in union" or "of one spirit." It's made from *unus*, or "one," and *animus*, meaning "breath," "life," or "spirit."

UNDERSTAND   *un-der-STAND*   *verb*

This word comes from the Old English *understandan*, meaning "to stand in the midst of," or to be surrounded by something. The idea was that if you understood an idea or concept, it was as if you were completely immersed in it, sort of like standing underwater to see the life beneath the surface.

UNICORN

YOON-ee-korn

noun

You can probably guess that the "uni" in "unicorn" comes from the Latin prefix meaning "one," but what about "corn?" It comes from a Proto-Indo-European root meaning "head" or "horn," which is also the root of words like "carrot," "cornucopia," and "corner." Together, "unicorn" means "one horn."

UNIQUE   *YOO-neek*   *adjective*

You are unique, one of a kind. No one else is exactly like you. This word originally comes from the Latin *unus*, meaning "one."

UNIVERSE   *YOON-iv-urss*   *noun*

This word refers to everything in our existence, beyond our planet and solar system and into infinity. It originally comes from the Latin *universus*, which was used to mean "all together," "entire," or "whole." It literally meant "turned into one." The base word *versus* could mean "turn," as in "bend" or "change."

UNREQUITED   *un-ree-KWITE-ed*   *adjective*

Many romances tell of unrequited love, or love from one person that isn't returned by the person they yearn for. "Requite" was an English word meaning "repay," and it was more common historically than it is today. "Requite" is made up of the Old French or Latin prefix *re-* and the Middle English word *quite*, which meant "to clear" or "to pay." Unrequited love would be love that you give or pay to someone else, but they don't give it back.

UNRULY   *un-ROO-lee*   *adjective*

To be unruly is to refuse to obey the rules. "Ruly," an English word from the 1400s, meant "disciplined" or "following the rules," especially describing someone who followed religious rules. "Ruly" and "rule" both come from the Latin *regere*, meaning "to straighten" or "to rule." The idea was that following the rules, or even "ruling" as a king or queen does, was like walking down a straight (and therefore good) path.

UPHOLSTER   *up-HOL-stur*   *verb*

To upholster a sofa or chair is to cover it in fabric and cushioning. A person who upholsters furniture is called an upholsterer. This job title evolved from an older one, an "upholdester." An upholdester not only covered and repaired furniture but also sold small pieces of furniture and other goods. The idea was that this person helped you "uphold" furniture, or make it last longer, by repairing it.

URGENT   *UR-jent*   *adjective*

Something urgent must be dealt with right away. The word comes from the Latin *urgere*, meaning "to press hard." Another word for "urgent" is "pressing," and both refer to problems that make you feel like you're under pressure until they're solved.

Example: The father made an urgent call to the doctor when his child was sick.

USHER   *UH-shur*   *noun/verb*

Today, an usher is someone who welcomes you into a place and helps you find your seat, maybe at a theater or a church. "Usher" can also be a verb—to open the door or usher someone down the aisle. It was first a word for a porter or doorman, someone who opened doors to admit people to see their employers. This word originally comes from the Latin *ostium*, meaning "door" or "entrance," which in turn is from *os*, meaning "mouth."

USURP   *yoo-SURP*   *verb*

To usurp something, usually the throne from a king or queen, is to take it by force without having the right to it and claim yourself as the new ruler or owner. It is formed by the Latin *usus*, meaning "a use," and *rapere*, meaning "to seize."

Example: His mom usurped the controller after he played video games for too many hours.

UTILITY   *yoo-TILL-it-ee*   *adjective/noun*

Anything that can be used is said to have utility. A hammer has the utility of driving nails into wood and other materials. Electricity and water in your house are called "utilities" because they are resources you use. This word means "usefulness," from the Latin *utilis,* meaning "usable." This word shares a root with "utensil."

UTOPIA

yoo-TOH-pee-ah   *noun*

A utopia is a place where everyone is perfectly happy and there are no problems like war, disease, or political conflict. The word comes from a book called *Utopia* by the English philosopher Thomas More. The book was about the imaginary island of Utopia, which was completely perfect, with moral people and laws that made everyone happy. The book was a satire, or a story poking fun at real societies with real problems. Utopia means "nowhere" or "no place." Thomas More made it up using the Greek words *ou*, or "not," and *topos*, meaning "place." He was making a joke, saying this perfect place is called "Nowhere" because no place is actually perfect.

UTTER

UHT-ur   *verb*

To utter a word is to say it. This word originally comes from the Old English *utan*, "to put out." When you utter or say something, you put it out into the world.

UVULA

YOO-vyoo-luh   *noun*

If you open your mouth wide and look in the mirror, you can see your uvula, the little part that dangles down in the back of your throat. It is named after the Latin *uvola*, meaning "a small bunch of grapes."

VOLCANO

Read more on page 223

V

VACANT   *VAY-kent*   *adjective*

Something that is vacant is empty, or not full. A house or room that is vacant has no one inside of it. You might have seen the sign "Vacancy" outside of a hotel. This means there are empty rooms—one is available for you! The word comes from the Latin *vacare*, meaning "to be empty."

VACCINE   *VAK-seen*   *noun*

A vaccine is a substance that contains a small amount of a virus. It's not enough to make you sick, but it is enough to teach your body how to fight it so you are able to resist getting sick from the same disease in the future. The first vaccine was developed in 1800 by a doctor named Edward Jenner, who used this method to prevent people from getting smallpox by injecting them with the cowpox virus. Thanks to the cowpox virus, the word "vaccine" comes from the Latin *vaccinus*, meaning "from cows." Around the world, vaccines have nearly eliminated many deadly diseases including polio, tetanus, and mumps.

VAGABOND   *VAGG-uh-bond*   *noun*

A vagabond is someone who doesn't have a permanent job or house but continually travels from place to place. It originally comes from the Latin *vagus*, meaning "wandering" or "undecided."

VALEDICTORIAN   *VAL-uh-dik-TOR-ee-an*   *noun*

The valedictorian of your class is usually the person who graduates with the highest grades. When you graduate high school and college, the valedictorian will give a speech called a "valediction" wishing everyone good luck on their next chapter. It comes from the Latin *valedicere*, meaning "to bid farewell." This is from the Latin *Vale!* meaning "Farewell!" and *dicere*, meaning "to say."

VALIANT

VAL-ee-ent   *adjective*

When you do something valiantly, you show great effort or courage. A valiant hero is someone who is fearless in the face of danger. This word originally comes from the Latin *valere*, meaning "to be strong." Over time it evolved into *valoir*, "to be worthy," as in a worthy opponent. It's important to know that to make a valiant effort, you don't always have to win or succeed.

Example: She made a valiant effort to win student body president. Even though she lost, her parents and teachers were very proud!

VAMPIRE

VAM-pyer   *noun*

Vampire myths are so old that the word's etymology isn't clear. We know that the legends originated in Slavic countries and that blood-drinking monsters have been in stories at least as far back as the twelfth century. We also know that "vampire" was adopted into English from the French *vampire*, but it isn't clear where it came from before that. One theory is that it is related to a very old word for "witch" in a language spoken in Russia.

VENOM

VEN-um   *noun*

Venom is the poisonous liquid that some types of creatures, such as certain spiders and snakes, can inject with a bite or sting. In animals, venom is used for hunting prey or for self-defense. The word is derived from the Latin *venenum*, meaning "poison" or "drug." However, its original meaning was probably a "love potion" used to charm someone!

VERTEBRATE   *VER-tuh-brett*   *noun*

A vertebrate is any animal with a spine or backbone. Mammals, birds, fish, and amphibians are all vertebrates. An invertebrate is an animal without a spine, like an insect or a mollusk. A vertebra is one of the bones in your spine, which is made of joints that are designed to bend. The word "vertebrate" comes from the Latin *vertere*, meaning "to turn" like a hinge.

VICTORY   *VIK-tor-ee*   *noun*

This word for any winning achievement was originally a military term. It came to English from the Old French *victorie*, which originally came from the Latin. The Latin, *vincere*, means "to conquer."

VILLAIN   *VILL-un*   *noun*

Today we think of villains as being the clever enemies of legendary heroes. Originally, it was a plain-old insult that high-ranking people would use to refer to people from "lower" classes. In Middle English, it was a negative word for a commoner, like a peasant or farmer. It comes from the Latin *villanus,* meaning "farmhand."

VIRTUOUS   *VUR-choo-us*   *adjective*

Someone virtuous behaves in a morally good way. In Greek and Christian philosophy, the four fundamental virtues, or qualities that make a person good, are prudence (wisdom, knowing right from wrong), courage, temperance (self-control), and justice (fairness). The word comes from the Latin *virtutem*, meaning "moral strength" or "goodness." The base word, *vir*, means "(hu)man," giving "virtue" the sense that it is what good people should strive for.

Example: The way she cared for her elderly grandmother was virtuous.

VIVID VIV-id *adjective*

Something vivid is very colorful, like a tropical parrot with bright red and blue feathers. It can also mean something very realistic and memorable, like a dream where you remember every detail. This word comes from the Latin *vividus*, meaning "spirited" or "full of life," from *vivus*, meaning "alive."

Example: His spirit was as vivid as the flowers in the field.

VOLCANO

vol-KAYN-oh

noun

Volcanoes are mountains formed by hot magma from beneath the earth's surface. They are named after Vulcan, the Roman "god of fire." It was originally the name of the active volcano Mount Etna, located in Sicily, Italy, but was later applied to all volcanoes. The name Etna probably comes from the Greek *aitho*, meaning "I burn."

VORTEX VOR-teks *noun*

A vortex is a word for a natural whirlpool in the ocean or anything with a similar swirling shape, like a tornado or the center of a hurricane. It comes from the Latin *vertere*, meaning "to turn."

WIZARD~WITCH

Read more on pages 227 and 228

W

WAFFLE   *WAFF-ull*   *noun/verb*

The batter-based griddle cake we call a waffle was adopted from Dutch, originally coming from a Proto-Germanic root meaning "web" or "honeycomb." Waffling can also be a word for changing one's opinion frequently, which probably comes from the Scottish *waff*, meaning "to waver" (to lean back and forth).

WALTZ   *WALTS*   *noun/verb*

A waltz is a type of three-step dance in which the partners turn around as they dance. The word comes from the Old High German word *walzan*, meaning "to turn" or "to roll."

WEIRD   *WEERD*   *adjective*

This word for something strange and unusual comes from the Old English *wyrd*, meaning "fate" or "destiny." It was often used to describe witches and other supernatural beings who had the power to control fate. Some Germanic and Greco-Roman mythological stories included a group of witchlike sisters, usually three women called "weird sisters" or the Fates, who were thought to have power over human destiny.

WEREWOLF   *WAIR-wulf*   *noun*

The "wolf" part of this word makes sense, but what does "were" mean? It comes from an Old English word, *wer*, meaning "man." It shares an ancient Proto-Indo-European root, also meaning "man," with other male-centric words like "virile," meaning "manly."

WHALE   *WAYL*   *noun*

This word comes from the Old English *hwæl*, which was originally a word for any kind of large sea animal, including walruses or enormous types of ocean-dwelling fish.

WIDDERSHINS   *WID-ur-shinz*   *adjective*

This Scottish word meant "counterclockwise," or opposite the direction of the sun's path across the sky. It comes from a Middle Low German word meaning "against the way" or "in the opposite direction." This direction was thought by some to be unlucky.

WIGGLE   *WIG-ull*   *verb*

To wiggle is to move your body and squirm around! All animals wiggle around. This word is thought to come from the Middle Dutch or German *wiege*, meaning "cradle," referencing its rocking, back-and-forth motion.

WIGWAM   *WIG-wahm*   *noun*

A wigwam was a type of dome-shaped house built by some Native American tribes. It comes from the Algonquian *wikewam*, which was a word for "dwelling." It literally meant "their house."

WILDEBEEST   *WILL-duh-beest*   *noun*

This animal, also called a gnu, is a type of antelope. The word "wilde-beest" was originally a South African Dutch word that means "wild ox."

WINDOW   *WIN-doh*   *noun*

In the medieval era, houses were designed for warmth and shelter, so there were no holes in the walls aside from the door. At that time, a window was a hole in the ceiling that let in light and let out smoke from a fire. The word literally means "wind eye," from the Old Norse *vindauga*.

WINTER   *WIN-tur*   noun

Depending on where you live, your winter could have snow, rain, or sun. Regardless of where you are, though, the weather is probably harsher than during other parts of the year. The word "winter" was adopted from Old English, but it originally comes from a Proto-Germanic root that probably meant "the wet season." The Anglo-Saxons used winters to measure their age and the passage of time. The related Old English word *ænetre* means "one-year-old," or literally "one winter old."

WISDOM   *WIZ-dum*   noun

The first part of this word shares an origin with "wise," which is from the Old English *wis*, meaning "learned," "experienced," or "cunning." The Old English word is said to derive from a Proto-Indo-European root meaning "to see." The ending *-dom* meant "judgment." Together, these parts give "wisdom" the meaning "experienced judgment."

WITCH

WICH

noun

This word refers to a powerful person who practices magic, usually a woman. It comes from the Old English *wicce*, which refers to sorcery.

WIZARD

WIZ-urd

noun

We tend to think of fictional characters like Harry Potter and Gandalf when we think of this word. But in the fifteenth century, it was a word for a real person—a philosopher or wise leader. It comes from the Middle English *wys*, meaning "wise." The word came to mean someone who practices magic in the 1550s. Around that time, the legends of King Arthur (very old stories from the fifth and sixth centuries) were being retold and rewritten in a new language. That probably made stories about enchanters like Merlin popular again, influencing the change in the word's meaning.

WORLD   *WURLD*   *noun*

Usually we consider the world to be the globe and all the countries on Earth. Before people understood astronomy, the "world," or the Old English *woruld*, meant "human existence," "the human race," or "a long period of time."

WRITE   *WRIYT*   *verb*

This is our modern word for putting words on paper. It comes from the Old English *writan*, meaning "to draw the shape of (something)" or to make a scratch in a surface. Before that, it came from a Proto-Germanic source meaning "tear" or "scratch," because some of the earliest documentation involved scratching tallies and symbols into wooden tablets.

X-RAY

Read more on page 230

X

XENOPHOBIA   *ZEEN-oh-foh-bee-ah*   *noun*

Xenophobia is the fear of "the other." It translates into mistreatment of people who are from other countries or cultures. It is made up of the Greek *xeno-*, meaning "foreign" or "other," and *phobia*, meaning "fear."

Example: Xenophobia harms people and squashes the beauty of diversity.

X-RAY
EKS-ray
noun/verb
The X in X-ray was inspired by mathematics. In algebra, X symbolizes any number that is unknown in an equation. The scientist who discovered this form of energy in the 1800s named it "X-radiation," after the fact that it was, at the time, an unknown type of radiation.

XYLOPHONE   *ZY-loh-fohn*   *noun*

A xylophone is a musical instrument made of wood or metal bars that makes sound when struck with a mallet. The word literally means "the sound of wood," from the Greek *xylon*, meaning "wood," and *phōnē*, meaning "sound."

YOGA

Read more on page 233

Y

YACHT   *YOT*   *noun*

Today, the word "yacht" usually reminds people of white luxury boats that are good for relaxing on during ocean vacations. But in the 1550s, a yacht had a much more exciting purpose. It was used to chase down pirates! It comes from the Dutch word *jachtschip*, which literally means "ship for chasing," from a Proto-Indo-European root meaning "to hunt."

YEAST   *YEEST*   *noun*

Yeast is a type of living fungus that is most commonly used to make bread. When you add water to dry yeast, it starts to form bubbles and rise. It comes from a Proto-Germanic source meaning "foam" or "froth."

YELL   *YELL*   *verb*

Originally spelled *giellan* in Old English, this word comes from a Proto-Indo-European root meaning "to call." It is related to the Old English *galan*, meaning "to sing."

YELLOW   *YELL-oh*   *adjective*

The name of this sunny color comes from a Proto-Indo-European root meaning "to shine."

YES   *YESS*   *adverb*

The word "yes" doesn't seem long enough to be a compound word (a word made up of two other words), but it surprisingly is. It comes from the Old English *gea*, meaning "so," and *si*, meaning "it is." Together they form *gise*, or "So be it!" It was used as a strong and eager form of agreement.

YIELD *YEELD* *noun/verb*

To yield in an argument is to give way to the other's wishes. To yield when you're driving is to wait while another car passes. In these examples, when you yield, you allow the other person to move ahead. Yield also means to produce or provide. It comes from the Old English *gieldan*, meaning "to pay, reward, or worship."

YIKES *YIYKS* *interjection*

"Yikes!" probably comes from *yoicks*, a call that eighteenth-century hunters would yell out while on the trail of a fox.

YODEL *YOH-dul* *verb*

Singers in the Alps who rapidly switch between high and low pitches. The technique name comes from the German *jodeln*, meaning "to utter the syllable 'jo.'" In German, "*jo*," pronounced "yo" in English, is an exclamation of joy.

YOGA

YOH-guh

noun

Many people take yoga classes today to relax, meditate, and build their physical strength. Originally a Hindi word meaning "union," it is used in the religions Hinduism, Buddhism, and Jainism to find peace. It comes from the Sanskrit *yuj*, meaning "to join" or "to unite."

YOUTH *YOOTH* *noun*

This word for a person in the early years of life is derived from a Proto-Indo-European source meaning "vital force" or "vigor"—basically "life energy."

ZOMBIE

Read more on page 237

Z

ZANY *ZAY-nee* *adjective*
Someone who is acting zany is behaving in a silly and exaggerated way. This word comes from the Italian theater style known as commedia dell'arte, or simply "Italian comedy," popular from the sixteenth to the eighteenth centuries. In this style, there were a few common character types that appeared in many plays and performances, wearing masks with exaggerated faces on them. One of them was Zanni, who was often a trickster or a silly jester type. His name is the origin of the word "zany" today.

ZEALOUS *ZELL-us* *adjective*
Someone who is zealous, or a zealot, is very passionate about their beliefs, sometimes to the point of being extreme. It comes from the Greek *zelos*, which described someone overly passionate and eager to fight for their beliefs. This is also the source of "jealous," and for some time, "jealous" and "zealous" were interchangeable.

ZEBRA *ZEE-bra* *noun*
Before it was a name for the striped animals we know as "zebras" today, this word referred to a type of wild donkey. The word comes from an African language, perhaps Congolese. Another word for the zebra was the Latin *equiferus*, meaning "fierce horse."

ZEITGEIST *ZIYT-GIYST* *noun*
This word refers to the overall mood of a culture during an era in history. For example, the zeitgeist during "the Renaissance" was inspired by progress, discovery, art, and new technological achievements. The word is German, meaning "spirit of the age" but literally translated as "time-spirit."

ZENITH   *ZEE-nuth*   noun

Zenith is a word for the highest point of something. For example, the "zenith of power" for the Roman Empire would be the moment when the Romans were at their most powerful. In astronomy, it can also mean the point directly over your head in the sky, or the highest point of a star or planet as it travels across the night sky ("at its zenith"). The word comes from the Arabic term *samt ar-ras*, meaning "the path over the head." When this term was translated into Medieval Latin, it was spelled *cenit* or *senit*, which became *cenith* in Old French before it evolved into modern French as *zénith* and into English as "zenith."

ZEPHYR   *ZEFF-ur*   noun

A zephyr is a light and refreshing breeze. It comes from the name of the Greek god Zephyros, who embodied the west wind. Zephyros's name comes from *zophos,* which meant both "the west" and also "the dark region" because the sun sets in the west.

ZERO   *ZEE-roh*   noun

Before the invention of mathematics, most languages had no word for "zero." The English word for it was adopted from French or Italian, both of which were from the Medieval Latin *zephirum*. But the Latin word comes from the Arabic *sifr*, or "cipher," which is the name of the symbol that was first used to note zero, or no quantity at all. "Cipher" is also a word for something written in code, because without knowing the code, the encoded message means nothing.

ZIGGURAT   *ZIG-oo-rat*   noun

A ziggurat is a huge, ancient Mesopotamian tower. It is similar to a pyramid but made of steps and built with a flat top. Ziggurats were often used as temples or had temples on top. The word comes from the Assyrian *zaqaru*, meaning "to be high."

ZIGZAG   *ZIG-zag*   *adjective/noun/verb*

This word was adopted from French but probably originally came from the German word *Zickzack*, from *Zacke*, meaning "tooth" or "prong." The earliest recorded use of this word in English was to describe garden paths that alternated in direction, but it is recorded in German as a description for military tactics.

ZODIAC   *ZOH-dee-ak*   *noun*

The zodiac is a circular area of the night sky that is divided into the twelve major constellations: Aries, Taurus, Gemini, Cancer, Leo, Virgo, Libra, Scorpio, Sagittarius, Capricorn, Aquarius, and Pisces. People use these star signs predict what might happen in the future. The word "zodiac" comes from the Greek *zodiakos kyklos*, meaning "the zodiac circle." It is literally translated as "circle of little animals."

Example: What is your zodiac sign? If you know your birthday, you can find out!

ZOMBIE

ZOM-bee

noun

Zombies, or corpses that have come to life again, first appeared in voodoo religion from cultures in the Caribbean and Louisiana. The word first meant "phantom" or "ghost" before monster movies in the early 1920s made flesh-eating zombies popular. The word most likely originally derived from the Kimbundu word *nzambi*, meaning "soul," but it could be from the Spanish *sombra*, meaning "shade" or "ghost."

ZOO   *ZOO*   *noun*

Zoology is a combination of the Greek *zoion*, meaning "animal," and *-logia*, meaning "study." The word "zoo" was a popular nickname for the London Zoological Gardens, which opened in 1826 and became the inspiration for many zoos around the world.

PART III

WORD
PLAY

A BELLY FULL OF WORDS

Cultures around the world showcase their amazing customs in different ways, and yet there's one thing everyone has in common: We love to eat! Our word "food" comes from the Old English *foda*, meaning "nourishment or fuel"—basically this can be anything that gives you energy and fulfills you.

Explore this list of delicious word histories and see if you can spot your favorite foods—or a food you've never heard of from another country. Without looking at the definition, see if you can guess which language that word comes from.

AMBROSIA: A fruit salad popular in the American South. It was named after the Greek and Latin *ambrosia*, the mythical food and drink enjoyed by the gods. It is from the Greek *ambrotos*, meaning "immortal."

BACON: From a Germanic word meaning "back meat." Originally considered food for working-class people—hence, you work hard to "bring home the bacon."

BAGEL: From the Yiddish word *beygl*, originally from the Old German *boug*, meaning "ring or bracelet." (In Old English, an Anglo-Saxon lord was called a *beaggifa*, or "ring-giver.")

BAGUETTE: A long, narrow French bread loaf, meaning "wand," "rod," or "stick" in French.

BANANA: Adopted directly from the language Wolof, which is spoken in the African countries Senegal and Gambia.

BARBECUE: From the Spanish *barbacoa*. The Spanish word originally came from the Arawakan word *barbakoa*, from Haiti. The word *barbakoa* is a framework of sticks for curing meat.

BEIGNET: A fried French pastry, from the Old French *buigne*, meaning "bump" or "lump."

BISCUIT: Originally from the Latin *panis bis coctus*, meaning "bread twice baked."

BROCCOLI: Adopted from Italian from *broccolo*, meaning "sprout."

BURRITO: From Spanish, meaning "little donkey." Named after the animal because it contains many different things, and a burro (donkey) can carry big packs filled with many things.

BUTTER: Thought to be derived from the Greek word *boutyron*, which literally means "cow-cheese."

CAULIFLOWER: Originally spelled *cole florye* in English, this word comes from the Italian *cavoli fiori*, meaning "flowered cabbage."

CEREAL: This word for the breakfast food, and for grains in general, gets its name from the goddess Ceres (known as Demeter to the Greeks), who represented agriculture, grains, fertility, and motherhood. Her name comes from a word meaning "to satiate, feed," also the source of "create" and "increase."

CHEESE: There are more than 1,000 different types of cheese produced all over the world using different methods. Many of them involve curdling and aging milk until it becomes a solid. The word "cheese" probably comes from a Proto-Indo-European root meaning "to ferment" or "to become sour."

CHIMICHURRI: From the Basque *tximitxurri*, which is loosely translated as "a mixture of several things in no particular order." The Basque language is spoken in certain areas of northern Spain and southwestern France.

CHOCOLATE: Originally an unsweetened Aztec drink made with cacao beans from the Aztecan word *chocola-tl*.

CHOP SUEY: A Chinese dish popular in the United States made of stir-fried meat and veggies. This is thought to be from the Taishanese *tsap seui*, meaning "odds and ends" or "miscellaneous leftovers."

CHOW MEIN: A Chinese word for stir-fried noodles. This is adapted from *chāu-mèing* in the Taishanese dialect, meaning "stir-fried noodles" or "sautéed noodles."

COCONUT: A nut of the coco tree, or palm tree, from the Spanish/Portuguese *coco*, meaning "a grinning face" because the three holes in coconut shells were thought to look like a face.

COFFEE: From the Arabic word for coffee, *qahwah*. This may have originally been from a word meaning "wine" or may have been from the name of the Kaffa region in Ethiopia where coffee was grown.

COOKIE: From the Dutch *koekje*, meaning "little cake."

COUSCOUS: A Maghrebi (North African / Moroccan) dish made of crushed durum wheat or other grains, originally from the Arabic *kaskasa*, meaning "to pound."

CROISSANT: Named for its shape, from Old French *croisant*, meaning "crescent of the moon."

CURRY: This spice blend is common in Indian, Asian, and Mediterranean cuisine. The word comes from Tamil (South Indian) *kari*, meaning "sauce" or "relish for rice."

ÉCLAIR: A long, oval-shaped pastry with cream filling. Its name comes from *éclair*, the French word for lightning bolt. The sweet treat, like lightning, is "long in shape but short in duration"—that is, so tasty that you can't help but eat it very quickly!

FALAFEL: Fried chickpea bites, from the Arabic word *falafil*, which means "crunchy."

FILET MIGNON: A small, tender cut of steak, from the Old French *filet*, meaning "thread" or "strip," and *mignon*, meaning "delicate," "dainty," or "cute."

FRUIT: This word originally comes from a Proto-Indo-European root meaning "to enjoy."

GARLIC: From Old English *garlec*, meaning "spear leek," named after the shape of the stalk that grows out of the bulb.

GUMBO: A thick soup containing meat, rice, and okra (a small, green, pod-shaped vegetable). The word is a Louisiana French term but probably comes from a Bantu (Central African) word meaning "okra."

HONEY: Possibly from a Proto-Indo-European root meaning "golden."

KETCHUP: Perhaps from the Chinese word *kôe-chiap*, meaning "brine of fish," or from the name of the Malaysian sauce called *kichap*, which was made with pickled fish and mushrooms.

KIELBASA: A Polish sausage. It is either from the Turkish word *kulbasti*, meaning "grilled cutlet" or literally "pressed on the ashes," or from the Hebrew word *kolbasar*, meaning "all kinds of meat."

KITCHEN: From the Latin *coquere*, meaning "to cook."

MACARONI: From the Italian word *maccaroni*, a word for a pasty food made of flour, cheese, and butter. In English in the 1700s, it was also a word for a fashionable, fancy young man (also called a "fop" or "dandy") because macaroni was a rare and fancy dish. (This is why Yankee Doodle "stuck a feather in his hat and called it macaroni.")

MARINATE: Originally meaning to pickle in ocean saltwater. It's from the Latin *marinus*, meaning "of the sea."

MARSHMALLOW: From the Old English *mersc-mealwe*, a plant that grows near marshes and whose roots were used to make early versions of these sweet treats.

MAYONNAISE: From French, but its exact origin isn't clear. It may have been named for a battle at the city of Mahón, Spain, or from *moyeu*, an older French word for "egg yolk." It could also be from the name of Charles de Lorraine, duke of Mayenne, who, according to legend, took the time to finish a dish of saucy chicken before a battle.

MOCHA: From the name of a seaport in southern Yemen where a type of coffee was exported. Now it's the name for coffee with chocolate syrup.

NACHOS: This dish of cheesy chips was supposedly invented in the Mexican town of Piedras Negras in the 1940s by a chef named Ignacio "Nacho" Anaya, after whom it was named.

ONION: From the Old French *oignon*, originally from the Latin *unionem*, which means "one" or "unity." In Latin, it referred to the visible layers of an onion that form one unified whole.

PIZZA: Adopted from Italian for any kind of cake, tart, or pie. Origin is uncertain, but it may be from the Greek *pitta*, meaning "cake" or "pie," or from a Germanic word meaning a "bite" or "morsel."

POMEGRANATE: A fruit whose insides are made up of juicy edible seeds, from the Medieval Latin *pomum granatum*, meaning "apple with many seeds."

QUICHE: An egg-based pie you might eat for breakfast, adopted from French. It originally comes from the German *Küche*, or "cake."

SAUSAGE: Before refrigerators and big grocery stores, people needed to preserve, or save, foods to eat during long winters. One way to save meat was to salt it and make it into sausage. This word originally comes from the Latin *salsus*, meaning "salted."

SAUTÉ: To cook something quickly in oil. From the French *sauté*, which literally means "jumped" or "bounced." The word was originally from the Latin *saltare*, meaning "to hop" or "to dance."

SHISH KEBAB: From the Turkish word *siskebap*, meaning "skewer of roast meat."

SHRIMP: Likely from the Old Norse word *skreppa*, meaning a thin person, due to their size and slim shape.

SPAGHETTI: Literally means "strings" or pieces of twine, adopted from Italian.

SQUASH: Borrowed from the Narragansett (Native American) word *askutasquash*, meaning "the things that may be eaten raw."

STROGANOFF: A Russian beef dish named after Count Pavel Stroganoff, a Russian diplomat and general who lived in France and enjoyed blended cuisines.

SUSHI: A Japanese sticky rice prepared with vinegar, usually served with fresh fish or veggies. The dish was preceded by *narezushi*, meaning "salted fish" that was stored in fermented rice.

SYRUP: Comes in part from the Old French *sirop*, meaning "sugared drink." But it is originally from the Arabic word *sharab*, "to drink."

TOFU: A protein-rich food made of solid soy milk. The word is adopted from Japanese, originally from Chinese *doufu*, meaning "rotten beans" or "fermented beans."

TOMATO: From the Aztec word *tomatl*, literally meaning "the swelling fruit."

TORTILLA: From Spanish, literally "a little cake."

TUNA: Also once called a "tunny," this type of fish probably gets its name from the Greek name *thynnos*, which literally meant "darter" from the way they move quickly in the water.

TUTTI-FRUTTI: The name of this ice cream and candy flavor was adopted from Italian and means "all fruits."

VEGETABLE: From the Old French *vegetable*, meaning "living," from the Medieval Latin *vegetabilis*, meaning "growing" or "flourishing."

VINEGAR: From the Old French *vinaigre*, literally meaning "sour wine."

WONTON: A square wrapper made of dough and filled with meat and/or veggies. Originally from the Mandarin *hun tun*, meaning "stuffed dumpling."

YOGURT: Originally a Turkish word whose source, *yog*, means "to condense."

ZUCCHINI: From the Italian *zucca*, meaning "gourd" or "squash."

NOW THAT'S AN EARFUL!

Music is a language we can all appreciate, no matter what country or culture it originates from. Even if you can't understand the words to a song in another language, you can enjoy how it sounds or the way it inspires you to move!

The word "music" was adopted from the Old French *musique*. It originally comes from the Greek phrase *mousike techne*, or "the art of the Muses." The Muses were Greek goddesses who inspired people to create music, poetry, art, stories, and other inventions. Music and poetry were thought to be some of the most important work of the muses.

Listening to new music is a fun way to experience different cultures. It's also a peek at magical sounds that vibrate around the world. The best part about music? The more we learn about it, the more we want to know.

ALTO: Originally a word describing a high, male singing voice. This is now a word to describe the lower ranges of women's singing voices. It comes from the Latin *altus*, meaning "high" or "grown tall."

ARIA: A song in an opera with one person singing. It's from the Italian *aria*, or *arietta*, meaning "air." The name refers to a light, simple style of playing and performing—like air.

BANJO: A musical instrument that looks like a circular, long-necked guitar. Probably named after the similar African instrument called the *mbanza*. It's also possible it was named after or influenced by a type of Portuguese instrument called a *bandore* or *bandurra* that also had a similar shape. In 1764, Thomas Jefferson wrote about a banjo but called it a "banjar."

BARITONE: A male singing or speaking voice lower than a tenor but higher than a bass, from the Greek *barytonos*, meaning "deep-toned" or "heavy-sounding."

BASS: The deepest or lowest sound range in music, from the Latin word *bassus*, meaning "short" or "low."

BLUES: The blues is an American music style that expresses sadness and melancholy (just like when you're "feeling blue"). It is inspired by African American spirituals and lived experiences. Part of the defining sound are the "blue notes" or "worried notes" that sound sad, giving the song that "blue" emotion.

CHOIR: First spelled *queor* and originally a word for the part of a church where the singers stood during services. It comes from the Latin *chorus*, meaning a group of singers. The current meaning became common in English around the year 1400.

CHORD: Two or more notes played at the same time to make a new, blended sound. It's a shortening of the word "accord," or an agreement. The word *corde* is also a Middle English word (*chorda* in Latin) for the string of a musical instrument, which probably influenced the meaning of the word.

CLARINET: A woodwind instrument with an opening shaped like a bell. It's from the French *clarinette*, meaning "little bell," originally from the Latin *clarus*, meaning "clear" or "bright."

CRESCENDO: An increase in the loudness of a song or musical piece, originally from the Latin *crescere*, "to grow or increase."

CYMBALS: Brass plates that make a ringing sound when they're crashed together. It originally comes from the Greek word *kymbe*, meaning "bowl" or "cup."

GLOCKENSPIEL: An instrument similar to a xylophone, but with steel bars instead of the xylophone's wooden bars. It was originally fashioned as a set of bells of different sizes. The term is adopted from German and translates to "play of bells."

GUITAR: From the French word *guitare*, originally from the Greek word *kithara*, a similar instrument with a triangular body and seven strings. It's possible that it is originally from the Persian *sihtar*, another similar instrument.

HARMONY: A collection of musical sounds played together to make chords. Although it was adopted from French, it originally came from the Greek *harmonia*, meaning "joining" or "agreement."

HIP-HOP: A musical style named for its rhythm and lyrical bars. It was developed by African American, Latino, and Caribbean communities in the Bronx, New York, in the 1970s.

LYRICS: The words to a song. This word was originally a name for a type of poem, adopted from the Middle French *lyrique*, written to be played as a song. In Latin, *lyricus* specifically meant one that could be accompanied by the musical instrument called a lyre.

MELODY: The melody of a song is the main part of it (the part you might hum when thinking about the song). This is compared to the harmony, which blends with the melody. It's also a word for any pleasant tune. It comes from the Greek *meloidia*, meaning "a singing," "a choral song," or a tune that goes with a lyric poem.

OPERA: A musical play in which all of the actors sing, from the Latin *operari*, meaning "to work."

ORCHESTRA: Today, this is a word for a collection of people playing instruments, or the area where they play beside a stage. In the 1600s and earlier, it was the area where a chorus of dancers would perform. It comes from the Greek *orkheisthai*, meaning "to dance."

PIANO: Originally called a pianoforte, it literally meant "soft loud." This instrument started out as a more complex version of the harpsichord. When it was invented around 1700, its inventor, Bartolomeo Cristofori, called it by the full Italian name, *gravicembalo col piano e forte*, meaning "harpsichord with soft and loud."

REGGAE: "The Reggay" was a dance style popular in Jamaica until 1968, when a song by the band Toots and the Maytals led to it becoming its own musical genre. The word may come from the term *rege-rege*, meaning "a protest" or "an argument."

RHYTHM: From the Greek *rhythmos*, which meant "measured flow or movement," or "symmetry."

SAXOPHONE: A woodwind instrument with a reed and a brass body. It comes from the name of its Belgian inventor, Adolphe Sax, plus the Greek *phonos*, meaning "sounding."

SOPRANO: The highest range of all singing voices. It means "high" in Italian, from the Latin *super*, meaning "above" or "over."

SYMPHONY: A long musical composition usually played by an orchestra. It was originally a word for any assortment of musical instruments played together. The English word is from the Old French *simphonie*, meaning "musical harmony." Originally, it was from the Greek *symphonos*, meaning "harmonious" or "agreeing in sound."

TEMPO: The speed of music, from the Italian word *tempo*, meaning "time." It is originally from the Latin *tempus*, meaning "time" or "season."

TENOR: A higher male singing voice, compared to baritone and bass. Adopted from the Old French *tenor*, a word for "meaning" or "substance." This word was given to the tenor voices because they usually sang the main melody of a song in medieval music.

TREBLE: The higher tones of sound. It's from the Old French *treble*, meaning "a third part." In medieval music, the treble was the third part above the melody, which was performed in the tenor range.

VIOLIN: An earlier version of the "violin" was called a *viola da braccio*, or "violin of the arm." This is because the bow looks like an extension of the arm. Its name comes from Vitula, a Roman goddess of joy. Her name is related to the Latin *vitulari*, meaning "to be joyful."

SONG EXPLORATION

Finally, let's take a look at the lyrics of the song "Twinkle Twinkle Little Star."

This popular song is sung to the same tune as the song "Baa Baa Black Sheep" and the alphabet song.

That tune comes from an earlier French folk song called *"Ah! vous dirais-je Maman,"* or "Oh! Shall I Tell You Mommy," about a child who wants candy. The famous composer Wolfgang Amadeus Mozart made the French tune even more popular by creating new versions of it in the 1780s. The lyrics we know today were written by poet and novelist Jane Taylor in 1806.

Take a look at the lyrics in the first verse of the song, and explore the origins below:

> *Twinkle, twinkle, little star,*
>
> *How I wonder what you are!*
>
> *Up above the world so high,*
>
> *Like a diamond in the sky.*
>
> *Twinkle, twinkle, little star,*
>
> *How I wonder what you are!*

DIAMOND: The word "diamond" refers to a very hard gemstone. It is derived from the Greek *adamas*, meaning "the hardest metal," or what we call "adamantium" in English. Adamantium is a legendary metal, supposedly the hardest substance in existence. You may recognize it if you're familiar with the X-Men superhero franchise, but adamantium appeared in fictional stories during or before the Middle Ages, many centuries before the X-Men were created. While diamond is a gemstone, it was given the name as well because it is the hardest known natural material.

SKY: This word was adopted from Old Norse, and it originally meant "cloud." Before that, the word for sky was *heofon*, or "heaven."

STAR: Spelled *steorra* in Old English, this is a very old word with a Proto-Germanic root that also meant "star."

TWINKLE: Stars seem to twinkle or sparkle and change in brightness in the night sky. That's because Earth's moving atmosphere makes the light from the star shift and refract as the planet turns. The word comes from the Old English *twincan*, meaning "to wink" or "to blink."

WONDER: A wonder is something marvelous and amazing. "Wonder" comes from the Old English *wundrian*, meaning "to be astonished" or "to admire."

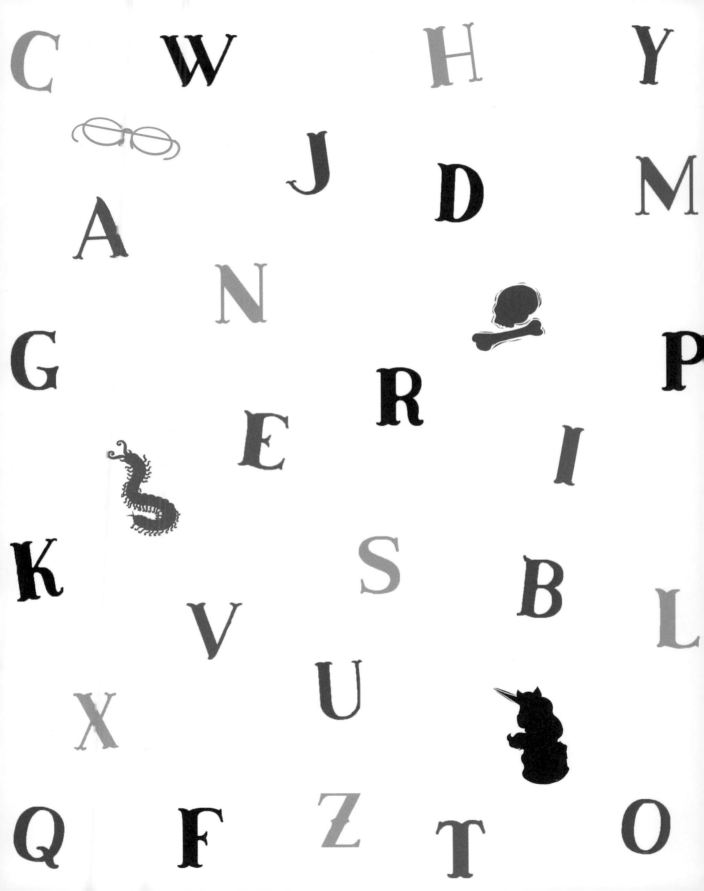

REFERENCES

It required more books and articles to write this book than there are entries in it. The principal sources used to produce it are as follows. These sources often disagree on the origins of words. I have attempted to select the origins that have the strongest consensus, but in some cases, I selected the most interesting (and often kid-friendly) theory. Some were used only as inspiration, while others form the core of each definition.

Many, many additional online and print sources were briefly consulted for supporting facts, sub-facts, and fact-checks, including Wiktionary and Wikipedia, both of which were multiply verified using the source materials from each article, as well as independent sources.

Ayto, John. *Dictionary of Word Origins: The Histories of More Than 8,000 English-Language Words.* New York: Arcade Publishing, 2011.

Barnhart, Robert K. *Barnhart Concise Dictionary of Etymology.* New York: HarperCollins, 2000.

Campbell, Lyle. *American Indian Languages: The Historical Linguistics of Native America, Volume 4 of Oxford Studies in Anthropological Linguistics.* New York: Oxford University Press, 2000.

Chapman, Robert L. *The Dictionary of American Slang, Subsequent Edition.* New York: Collins Reference, 1998.

Cresswell, Julia. *Oxford Dictionary of Word Origins (Oxford Quick Reference).* 2nd ed. New York: Oxford University Press, 2010.

Everett-Heath, John. *The Concise Dictionary of World Place-Names (Oxford Quick Reference).* New York: Oxford University Press, 2005.

Harper, Douglas. "Online Etymology Dictionary: Origin, History and Meaning of English Words." *Online Etymology Dictionary | Origin, History and Meaning of English Words.* Accessed September 27, 2019. etymonline.com.

Klein, Ernest. *Klein's Comprehensive Etymological Dictionary of The English Language.* Elsevier Publishing Company, 1971.

Lewis, Charlton Thomas. *An Elementary Latin Dictionary.* Harper & Brothers, 1895. Retrieved from Internet Archive website: https://archive.org/details /anelementarylat01lewigoog/

Liddell, Henry George., et al. *A Greek-English Lexicon.* New York: Clarendon, 1996.

Merriam-Webster.com. Merriam-Webster, 2019.

Onions, Charles T. *The Oxford Dictionary of English Etymology.* New York: Clarendon Press, 2006.

Skeat, William Walter. *Principles of English Etymology.* New York: Clarendon Press, 1887. Retrieved from Internet Archive website: https://archive.org /details/principlesofeng01skeauoft

Tolkien, J. R. R. *The Fellowship of the Ring: Being the First Part of The Lord of the Rings.* George Allen & Unwin, 1954.

Weekley, Ernest. *Etymological Dictionary of Modern English (A–K).* New York: Dover Publications, 1967.

Weekley, Ernest. *Etymological Dictionary of Modern English (L–Z).* New York: Dover Publications, 1967.

The World Factbook. Central Intelligence Agency, 2019. Accessed September 27, 2019. https://www.cia.gov/library/publications/the-world-factbook/

ACKNOWLEDGMENTS

For the inspiration and motivation needed to write this book—not to mention the ideas for many of the words included in it—I would like to offer special thanks to Andrew Zaferis, Emily Hightower, and Melissa Farris.

For spurring my interest and curiosity in this subject, I would like to recognize Douglas Harper, creator of The Online Etymology Dictionary.

For helping me transform this book from a tangle of research into a polished, kid-friendly resource, I would like to thank Erin Nelson and Constance Santisteban. For technical support and expertise, I would like to thank Lee Anderson and Dylan Moore.

For additional encouragement, knowledge, and advice, I would like to thank Jim and Kathy Farris, Bill and Lynn Farris, Marian Allen, Jeanne Bowerman, Tyler Moss, Zachary Petit, Shelby Garrett, Bernadine Marsis, the Gotham Ghostwriters team, the HOW+PRINT team, the *Writer's Digest* team, my educators at St. Mary's Episcopal School, DePaul University, and the University of Colorado Boulder, and all of my other family, friends, and colleagues who have patiently listened to me prattle on about word origins for the last decade or so.

ABOUT THE AUTHOR

An award-winning innovator of digital and print content and marketing solutions, and a prolific online and print journalist, Jess Zafarris has been writing about etymology for more than ten years, at UselessEtymology.com and on Twitter @UselessEty. Her professional roles have included working as executive director of marketing and communications for Gotham Ghostwriters, digital content director and content strategist for *Writer's Digest* and *ScriptMag*, editor-in-chief of *HOW Design* magazine, and online content director of *HOW* and *PRINT* magazines. Her articles and features have appeared in publications including *Writer's Digest*, *The Hot Sheet*, the *Denver Business Journal*, ABC News, and the *Memphis Commercial Appeal*. She has done freelance content development and audience engagement consulting for several major brands. She has an MA in journalism and mass communications and a BA in English literature.